COMMUNISM, THE COLD WAR AND THE FBI CONNECTION

Time to Set the Record Straight

by
Herman O. Bly
Special Agent of the FBI

Huntington House Publishers

Copyright © 1998 Herman O. Bly
All rights reserved. No part of this book may
be reproduced without permission from the
publisher, except by a reviewer who may quote brief
passages in a review; nor may any part of this book
be reproduced, stored in a retrieval system or copied
by mechanical photocopying, recording or other
means, without permission from
the publisher.

Huntington House Publishers
P.O. Box 53788
Lafayette, Louisiana 70505

Library of Congress Card Catalog Number 98-71671
ISBN 1-56834-149-5

Dedication

To my wife, Martha,
my best friend
and love of my life
for the past 60 years.

*To Dr. Bucks Miller
Chairman Dept Political science
With Best Wishes
Herman O. Bly
12/18/99*

*Compliments from
Linda Pilcher*

CONTENTS

Preface		ix
Acknowledgements		xi
One	I Become a Special Agent of the FBI	13
Two	The Dual Role of the FBI	19
Three	Early History of Communism	23
Four	Communist Manifesto	27
Five	The First and Second Internationals	31
Six	The Bolshevik Take-Over of Russia	33
Seven	The Communist International	37
Eight	Joseph Stalin Wins Soviet Power Struggle	41
Nine	Soviet International Conferences	45
Ten	Ideological Dispute	49
Eleven	World Strength of the Communist Party Organizations	53
Twelve	Soviet Manual: "Fundamentals of Marxism-Leninism"	57

Thirteen	Marxism-Leninism= Death and Human Suffering	61
Fourteen	The Break-Up of the Soviet Union: The Gorbachev Connection	65
Fifteen	Communism vs. Religion	69
Sixteen	Communism in the United States— 1919-1929	73
Seventeen	Communist Party, USA— 1930-1945	77
Eighteen	The Decline of the CP USA— 1945-1959	83
Nineteen	CP USA—1959-1996	93
Twenty	The FBI in the Forefront	101
Twenty-One	Franklin Delano Roosevelt Administration	107
Twenty-Two	FBI Thwarts the First Clandestine Group of Soviet Atom Spies	115
Twenty-Three	Harry S. Truman Administration	127
Twenty-Four	Dwight D. Eisenhower Administration	135
Twenty-Five	The Pros and Cons of the Counterintelligence Program Cointelpro	141
Twenty-Six	John F. Kennedy Administration	147

Contents

Twenty-Seven	Lyndon Baines Johnson Administration	153
Twenty-Eight	Richard M. Nixon Administration	159
Twenty-Nine	Gerald R. Ford Administration	165
Thirty	Jimmy (James Earl) Carter Administration	169
Thirty-One	Ronald Reagan Administration	179
Thirty-Two	George H. Bush Administration	189
Thirty-Three	International Corporate Aid for Marxist-Leninist Communism	195
Appendix A	Communist Party USA Organizational Structure	203
Appendix B	Conditions of Admission to the Communist International	207
Appendix C	Captive Nations as of 1982	215
Appendix D	Damage to U.S. Intelligence Agencies Endangers National Security	217
Epilogue		223
Bibliography		235

PREFACE

This book was written with a three-fold purpose. It strives to provide all pertinent information about the evils of Marxist-Leninist-Maoist communism and its four "sainted" leaders: Marx, Lenin, Stalin, and Mao.

Second, it provides a commentary on the ill-advised policy decisions of the Roosevelt, Truman, Kennedy, Johnson, Nixon, Ford, and Carter administrations, which aided the growth of communism and elevated a relatively undeveloped country of the 1930s (the Soviet Union) to the status of the most dangerous enemy our country and the Free World has ever faced. More than 160 Western corporations helped in the build-up of the economy and war capability of the Soviet Union from the 1930s to the 1980s.

Finally, it is time for everyone to understand and appreciate the role of the Federal Bureau of Investigation (FBI) in combating the subversive efforts of Marxist-Leninist communism during the cold war. While countries were being subjugated by the Soviet Union or revolutionary Communist parties throughout the world, the FBI contained the efforts of the Communist party, in the U.S. in its attempt to bring about a Soviet America.

This book is long overdue. Communist sympathizers and uninformed Americans believe that because of the fragmentation of the Soviet Union, communism is now dead. Dedicated Communist leaders are still in control of the People's Republic of China, with 1.2 billion people, as well as North Korea, Vietnam, and Cuba. If one out of every four people in the world live under Communist dictatorships, communism is far from dead.

I fear that what is past in our relations with the former Soviet Union may be a prologue in our relations with the People's Republic of China unless the American people and government leaders learn from the story of the twentieth-century "red plague."

ACKNOWLEDGMENTS

I am grateful to so many of my friends who have given me moral support and encouragement in the momentous task of writing this book. My wife's nurse, Norma Vary, was the first to encourage me to write and loaned me her electric typewriter to get started. Thanks to two sisters, Lavonne Webber and Goldie Goertzen, part-time nurses for my wife, who introduced me to the world of computers by lending me their IBM. This book certainly could not have been completed without Patricia Beall, the dedicated, unflappable computer operator who typed the manuscript. Thanks also to three computer experts who kept the computer operating: Keith and Pam Jansen and Tony Margullo.

Other indispensable people who helped with cogent advice on the subject matter were Dr. Michael Hansinger, former Lt. Col. of the U.S. Air Force with a deep understanding of Soviet intelligence operations; Otto Otepka, former Deputy Director of the Office of Security of the U.S. State Department; Douglas L. Waldorf, former FBI Agent and retired attorney; and Dr. Irvin D. Solomon, History Program Director, Florida Gulf Coast University.

Finally, credit should also be given to the former Special Agents of the FBI who blazed the trail ahead for me by writing important books for the American people, the more recent titles being: *The FBI - KGB War*, by Robert J. Lamphere (1986) and *Hoover's FBI*, by Cartha D. DeLoach (1995).

Thanks to Patricia G. Solley, Unit Chief, Office of Public and Congressional Affairs of the Federal Bureau of Investigation, for the review of my manuscript and for interposing no objections to its publication.

Thanks also to John Hollister Hedley, Ph.D., Chairman of the Publications Review Board of the Central Intelligence Agency, for the review of my manuscript and for interposing no objection to its publication. Dr. Hedley suggested that the following disclaimer appear in the book: "CIA's Publication Review Board had reviewed the manuscript for this book to assist the author in eliminating classified information and poses no security objections to its publication. This review however, should not be construed as an official release of information, confirmation of its accuracy, or an endorsement of the author's views."

Thanks also to Mickey Rosen who designed the original cover for my manuscript.

Thanks also to Professor Harvey Klehr, Department of Political Science, Emory University, for his 1992 book *The American Communist Movement, Storming Heavens Itself,* which provided help in preparing chapter 19 of this book, involving old-left and new-left organizations during the 1960s to 1980s.

ONE

I Become a Special Agent of the FBI

From the age of nine, my desire was to become a lawyer. My 1932 Handley High School year book description reads "hopes to be a lawyer." My father's languishing death from a brain tumor in 1933 delayed me going into law school for two years. I had two younger brothers who needed my support in order to graduate from high school. They graduated in June 1935, and in September 1935, I went to Washington, D.C. to study law. I was fortunate to find employment at the Washington Gas Light Co., and I worked during the day and went to law school six nights a week. I earned my LLB degree in June 1938 from National Law University, which merged with George Washington University following World War II. I passed the District of Columbia Bar Examination in the spring of 1939.

On 1 September 1939, the infamous Stalin-Hitler non-aggression pact opened the way for the partition of Poland. The Germans attacked Poland from the West and, three weeks later, the Soviets invaded Poland from the East. This was the beginning of World War II.

I tried to put my life in proper perspective. I recalled that one of my classmates at law school had been a fingerprint specialist of the Federal Bureau of Investigation (FBI), and he had suggested that I become an FBI Special Agent. I knew that one of the requirements for Special Agent was to be a lawyer; I also understood that I would be using my legal credentials and, at the same time, be of help to my country in a time of world upheaval which seemed to get more explosive day after day. In the spring of 1940, I submitted my application to the FBI, with my fingers crossed; I was told that, at that time, only one out of a thousand applicants achieved the position of Special Agent.

In early August 1940, after an extensive investigation of my past history, including a pretext interview with my mother by an agent, I received the important telegram instructing me to report to FBI headquarters in Washington, D.C. on 12 August 1940. I found myself in a seven-week training course, designated as "Class #7," with 26 aspiring special agents. We were alphabetically arranged in class sessions, and the man to my left was an attorney from Atlanta, Georgia. The man to my right was the former Dean of a Texas law school. We were each issued two large manuals: *Rules and Regulations* and *Manual of Instruction*. We were tested on the contents of these manuals, with the passing grade set at 85%. The FBI was then investigating over 100 federal crimes. We were required to know the basics of each of these investigations.

Most of the seven weeks of training were held at the FBI Academy and Firearms Range at the Marine Base at Quantico, Virginia. The hours of training were from 9 A.M. to 5 P.M. and 7 P.M. to 9 P.M. five days a week. We also trained from 9 A.M. to 1 P.M. on Saturday and 1 P.M. to 5 P.M. on Sunday. The instruction that impressed me most during the training was the four hour lecture on communism. Five-and-one-half years later, I would be giving the same lecture to new agents at the FBI Academy.

Only nineteen men graduated out of our class of twenty-six. I was one of the lucky nineteen who received his special agent credentials, the FBI badge and Colt 38 revolver. We were warned of the dire consequences of losing any of these items. Class #7 brought the number of special agents in the entire country to 1,000 for the first time.

My first office assignment was to the Chicago Field Office. I was the second special agent to be sent to such a large field office as Chicago. The first agent had been a graduate of Class #6, graduating a week earlier, and he had unfortunately been killed on the plane that also killed Senator Lundeen, on the way to the Chicago airport.

My wife, Martha, and I had been living in a one-bedroom apartment in the Rhode Island Gardens in Washington, D.C. The government was not, at that time, paying for transfer of furniture, so we sold all our furniture at almost give-away prices. We loaded our few remaining possessions in the trunk of our car and headed for Chicago in mid-October 1940. In Chicago, we rented a one-room apartment in a northside apartment hotel near Lake Michigan. The following Monday morning, at about 8:00 A.M., I reported for duty at the FBI Chicago field office.

Special Agent in Charge (SAC) Devereaux was already in his office and I was ushered in to see him at about 8:30 A.M. After welcoming me aboard and exchanging pleasantries, SAC Devereaux asked "Do you drive?"

When I said, "yes," he told me he had an assignment for me.

"I have a film which has to be in Springfield before noon, as an agent is speaking at a meeting and he needs the film for his lecture," Devereaux said. I took the film under my arm and obtained instructions from the Chief Clerk about how to sign out a car from the FBI garage several blocks away. I signed a 1940 Ford with a Mercury engine just after 9:00 A.M. At this point, I learned that Springfield was 150 miles away; I had less that three hours to make the trip on a two-lane highway. Although, I had to drive as fast as eighty-five miles per hour on the straight stretches, I managed to arrive at the Courthouse at 11:45 A.M. The agent was waiting for me on the steps. As I handed him the film, he thanked me and hurried inside. I had completed my first FBI field assignment, just under the wire, and I began to breathe a little easier.

After hurrying back from Springfield to the Chicago FBI field office, I received thirty-five assignment cards from the Chief Clerk, requiring full investigations of new cases, plus twenty lead cards. These lead cards concern investigations ordered by other field offices. They may require one inquiry, or more in-depth, detailed investigation. Each of these cases had to have some investigative activity each month or they were deemed delinquent. I found out that there were only twenty-nine special agents in the Chicago office with similar work loads covering northern Illinois as well as the Chicago area. The next morning, I was sent with an older agent on a one-week road trip to cover leads outside Chicago. He stayed with me for two days, after which I was on my own.

When I got back to Chicago, I found that my wife had exchanged our hotel apartment for another from which we had a view of Lake Michigan. Wives of special agents in the early 1940s had to fend for themselves, as they seldom saw their husbands until late at night. Happily, the wives were very helpful to each other. During the three months I was assigned to the Chicago office, my wife and I had evening meals together only on weekends.

My investigative work in Chicago was widely varied. I handled cases of bankruptcy, surveys of defense plants to discover and correct possible sabotage or espionage weaknesses, and cases involving subversives, including one troublesome Trotskyite Communist group that published a paper called "The Fighting Worker." I developed contacts in the "Red Squad" of the Chicago Police Department, a special unit set up to collect information on Communist and other subversive activities.

In February 1941, I was transferred to the St. Louis field assignment; three months was the average time a new agent was allowed to spend in his first office. In St. Louis, I was given some important cases to investigate, including the case against Ralph Shaw, the chairman of the Missouri District of the Communist Part, USA (CP USA). . There were also many naturalized Germans living in the St. Louis area, so we had to investigate a number of subjects with pro-Nazi sympathies, and there were pro-German organizations to investigate. The individual investigations were to determine the potential danger posed to our government by Hitler's threat against Europe. There were only seventeen agents in the St. Louis field office to cover all the federal cases and security problems in the state of Missouri.

In early October 1941, I received a teletype transfer to the New York field office. One week later, my wife and I were in New York City and, with hope running out due to the shortage of housing, we found a one bedroom apartment in Queens, Long Island. My assignment was the Security Squad, which handled Communist and other subversives threatening the U.S. government. The Squad developed the "Security Index" of individuals who were deemed dangerous to the U.S. government. Three hundred special agents in the New York office were assigned to handle all the federal violations and security problems in New York City and lower New York State.

Most people do not know that the U.S. government made no payment to special agents for overtime until about 1948, and even then agents were paid for a maximum of one-hour-and-twenty-minutes per day overtime. During the war years, I averaged from two to five hours a day overtime, and until my retirement in 1963, two to three hours a day overtime. The annual starting salary for Special Agents in 1940 was $3,200.00 per year. Factoring in the overtime the salary was less than $2.00 per hour. What a difference fifty-seven years make!

TWO

The Dual Role of the FBI

From May 1924, when J. Edgar Hoover was appointed Director of the FBI, until 1936, the Bureau's activities were strictly limited to investigations of violations of federal laws under rigid rules of evidence and procedure. In 1936, President Franklin D. Roosevelt added a dual role to the FBI's responsibilities: counterintelligence (CI) operations. The FBI thus became further responsible for the internal security of the United States.

On 24 August 1936, Director Hoover was summoned alone to the White House and Roosevelt told him, "I called you over because I want you to do a job for me and it must be confidential." Roosevelt said he wanted a broad intelligence picture of Communist and Fascist activities in relation to the economic and political life of the country. After discussing the president's request with the secretary of state and the attorney general, Director Hoover issued instructions to agents in FBI field offices to gather the required information. With two years of experience, Hoover outlined the general scope of this counter-intelligence effort in a memorandum to the attorney general. On 20 October 1938, the attorney general forwarded Hoover's memorandum to Roosevelt, who, during a personal meeting with Hoover on 2 November 1938, approved the approach and scope of the FBI intelligence effort.

On 26 June 1939, Roosevelt sent a confidential directive to cabinet members stating that investigation of all espionage, counter-espionage, and sabotage activities would be controlled and handled only by the FBI, the

Intelligence Divisions of the War Department, and the U.S. Navy. Other agencies were directed to report subversive activities to the nearest office of the FBI. The efforts of the FBI, the War Department, and the Navy were coordinated by a committee, headed by Hoover, called "The Interdepartmental Intelligence Conference." To facilitate the coordination, the conference adopted a series of "delimitation agreements," specifically defining the areas within which each organization would operate.

On 1 September 1939, following his non-aggression pact with Stalin, Hitler started World War II by attacking Poland. Roosevelt issued a public directive on 6 September 1939, which stated in part:

> I request all police officers, sheriffs, and all other law enforcement officers in the United States promptly to turn over to the nearest representative of the Federal Bureau of Investigation any information obtained by them relating to espionage, counter-espionage, sabotage, subversive activities, and violations of the neutrality laws.

This was the first public acknowledgment that the FBI was engaged in such CI activities as "counter-espionage" and investigation of "subversive activities." Subsequent directives of the same nature were issued by Roosevelt on 8 January 1943, by Truman on 24 July 1950, and by Eisenhower on 15 December 1953. From mid-1940 to 1946, under a decree signed by Roosevelt, the FBI was also made responsible for foreign intelligence work in the entire Western hemisphere. Coverage of the rest of the world, "as and when necessity arises," was assigned to the Military and Naval Intelligence branches.

You have briefly been introduced to the FBI which, in 1939, was given the awesome task of protecting the internal security of the United States. Is it any wonder that the FBI took such a strong investigative interest in communism? In 1917, the Communist Bolshevik Revolution overtook Russia, about one-sixth of the land surface of the world. By 1972, the International Communist Movement had taken control of over fifty countries, a third of the peoples of the world, and a quarter of the world's land surface. This was the beginning of communism, which developed into a 20th Century "red plague" that caused the deaths of 50,000,000 people. The FBI worked to contain the efforts of the Communist Party, USA (CP USA), inside the United States. This is the unbelievable story of the Cold War and how the International Communist Movement was able to achieve its phenomenal success through support from unusual sources and lack of opposition from sources that should have provided strong resistance to the sinister takeovers of defenseless countries.

THREE

Early History of Communism

Communism reaches back far in the political thought of man. Plato (427-347 B.C.), the Greek writer and philosopher, envisioned a Communist-type state in "On the Ideal State." Since Plato, every generation has had some student or thinker who has either been affected by, or has worried about, the social consequences of private property ownership in production of goods, and has sought to find some remedy through the abolition of private property.

The Communist movement began to slowly develop during the 18th century. Countries in Europe, including France, were undergoing a period of absolutism with "The Divine Right of Kings" as a prevailing concept. During the 18th century, a group of students turned their thoughts to the question of rights of man. Among these students were the French Encyclopedists, Rousseau and Diderot. These students felt that the evils in existence were primarily of a political nature rather than a political or economic nature, since the industrial age had not yet arrived.

The Industrial Revolution, which began in England and spread across the western part of the world, brought about economic changes and a new way of thinking. People went into factories and class consciousness became more distinctive and noticeable. The bourgeoisie (the employer or monied class) was sharply distinguished from the proletariat, or the working class.

Economic and social conditions continued to deteriorate. Bad living conditions, low wages, long working hours, and poor standards of living were effects of the Industrial Revolution. Men began to protest.

Robert Owen, an Englishman, endeavored to establish two model collective communities, one in England and one in New Harmony, Indiana. The French Utopian, or Utopian Socialists, began to make their appeal to the government and to the wealthy. Other groups with similar, yet diverse, approaches to the problem of the Industrial Revolution developed in other European countries.

Then in France, in 1789, an event occurred which formed a general protest to the political inequality existing there: the French Revolution was essentially a democratic revolution brought about by the bourgeoisie, not by the proletariat. This ultimately led to the partial overthrow of absolutism all over Europe, but intervening was the Napoleonic era which temporarily reinstated absolutism.

With the re-establishment of the new era of absolutism ("The Divine Right of Kings"), secret societies in Europe grew up and became the means of expression against absolutism and government by dictatorship. Some of these societies were revolutionary in character, while others were more moderate.

Karl Marx was born on 8 May 1818 in Prussia, the son of a middle-class Jewish family converted to Christianity. Marx himself, however, developed into an atheist. He attended three universities and studied law and philosophy. He earned a doctorate in science.

It is said that Marx was influenced by the Doctrine of Dialectical Materialism promoted by Hegel. This Doctrine of Dialectical Materialism is the cause and effect evident in every phase of life. The philosophy consists of a strictly materialistic concept of the universe and a conception of the nature of all movement and processes of all things in nature and society as being in the process of change and development. Applied to the history of human society, dialectical materialism is said to show that no system has endured forever, and that each system by which society has been organized contained the seeds of its own destruction. Each system has gone down before a new system, and each succeeding system has marked a higher stage of development and advance in human freedom. Thus, the capitalistic state, at its inception, brought into existence a new class, the proletariat, which, according to those who follow the tenets of dialectical materialism, will eventually destroy capitalism. There is a contradiction between private ownership and socialized production, involving a struggle between opponents which cannot be resolved until socialism takes place.

Even today, dedicated Communists still believe that the capitalist system is in the last stages of decay and is ready to be replaced by the "dictatorship of the proletariat." The dictatorship of the proletariat will in turn be replaced by the ultimate attainment: utopian socialism.

After completing his education, Marx acquired a German newspaper, the *Rheinische Zeitung*. The paper, because of its radical articles by Marx and Friedrich Engels, was suppressed and Marx was exiled from Prussia to Paris in 1843. In Paris, Marx became associated with two "liberal thinking" organizations: the Young Hegelians (proponents of dialectical materialism) and the Doktoren Club (where he first got to know Engels, who became a lifelong friend).

Engels was born in 1820 in Prussia, to a well-to-do family of merchants. He was highly educated and it is said that by age twenty-five, he knew twenty-six languages.

France was at this time the seat of revolutionary liberal thought, since liberal thought had been suppressed in the rest of Europe. The first revolutionary organization, called The League of Exiles, was founded in 1834, and was composed of artisans, or skilled workers, and intellectuals. It was the first organization to unite groups of different nationalities dedicated to the overthrow of existing governments. The League of Exiles broke up in 1836, with the intellectuals going in one direction and the artisans going in another.

A second revolutionary organization under the leadership of Wilhelm Weitling, founded and was called The League of the Just. The League of the Just became the most important of the secret societies, and between 1836 and 1847, both Marx and Engels were urged to join. Both declined however, because they did not want to affiliate themselves with any organization which was unlikely to achieve a revolutionary program.

FOUR

Communist Manifesto

Blueprint of Communism Comes to Life

In 1848, in light of the revolutionary spirit in Europe, Marx and Engels agreed to join the League of the Just on the following conditions: that the name be changed to the Communist League; that the organization cease to be conspiratorial (underground) and become openly agitational; that the league would publish a statement of its aims and purposes.

These conditions were agreed to, and, as a result, the "Communist Manifesto" was issued in January 1848. This forty-eight-page manifesto was prepared by Marx, with the assistance of Engels. It became one of the most thought-provoking documents of all times, forming the basis of Communist theory and providing a blueprint for communism. The manifesto was written in simple language, but contained the most profound revolutionary doctrine.

In order to assist the reader in better understanding Communist theory, the following outline is a combination of Marxist philosophy and the philosophy contained in the Communist Manifesto:

> The Marxist philosophy is a philosophy of history. The primary moving force in any social change is the system of economic production which is in operation at any given time. Marxists believe that law, religion, politics and philosophy are all arrived at through the reaction of the human mind

to the methods which are used by society to obtain the necessary means of life. Marxists believe that whoever controls production occupies a place of importance and special power.

The Marxist concept of economics is that production should be used for necessity rather than profit and the capitalist system, in obtaining profits, exploits labor (the working class). Marxists believe that private property rights should be abolished and all property should be owned by the state. Capitalism, as it exists today, is dying because of its desire for profits and the resulting overproduction and under consumption. Marxists claim that capitalism, in its desire to increase profits both by obtaining raw material and by opening new markets, creates imperialism, which, in turn, causes wars.

To the Marxist, the state is regarded as an economic organization, established for the benefit of capitalists and for the exploitation of the working class. The state, however, is a political organization to be used by the Communists to protect the working class. Voting rights and other God-given rights should not be routinely provided to the working class as means of obtaining socialism, since the working class is never in possession of all the facts. The government in a Marxist society should be in the hands of the enlightened few (selected by the Communists), who will accomplish what the working class would want if they were in possession of all the facts. The capitalist form of government must be overthrown and captured by the proletariat. Once it is captured, it can be transformed into a dictatorship by the enlightened few who are in power in the Communist party. Then it can progress toward socialism.

The Communist Manifesto proposed the following ten points for ultimate change of a capitalist country into a Communist state:

1. Abolition of private property and the application of rent from land for public purposes,
2. A heavy progressive or graduated income tax,
3. Abolition of all right of inheritance,
4. Confiscation of the property of all emigrants and rebels,
5. Centralization of credit in the hands of the state by means of a national bank with state capital and an exclusive monopoly on banking,
6. Centralization of the control of communication and transportation in the hands of the state,
7. The adoption of a common plan to extend the means of production,
8. An equal obligation of all to work, with the establishment of industrial armies, especially for agriculture;
9. Combination of agriculture with manufacturing industries and the gradual abolition of the distinction between the town and the country by a more equal distribution of the population,
10. Free education, the abolition of child labor "in its present form," and the combination of education with industrial and technical training.

A number of the above points appear to be sound, both economically and socially, especially to "liberal thinkers," and that is undoubtedly what attracted many to Marxism. What was less evident was the despicable manner by which these points would be applied and practiced by the Communists, or any other dictatorial group.

The closing words of the *Communist Manifesto* are:

> The Communists disdain to conceal their views and aims. They openly declare that their ends can be attained only by the forcible overthrow of all existing social conditions. Let the ruling class tremble at a Communist revolution. The proletarians have nothing to lose but their chains. They have a world to win. Working men of all countries unite.

From 1848, the *Communist Manifesto* was printed in many languages, circulated in many countries, and eagerly read by liberal and revolutionary individuals.

FIVE

The First and Second Internationals
1864-1918

The First International (1864, London)
Groups of workers met at an international exposition in England in 1862 and made plans to hold an international conference to be held in London in 1864. The 1864 Conference was held, as scheduled, and became known as "the First International," or the "International Association of Working Men."

Although Karl Marx was instrumental in the creation of the First International, all delegates were not Marxists and did not adhere to his revolutionary views. Those attending the First International Conference in London in 1864 included the Lassalleians (followers of Ferdinand Lassalle, 1825-1864). This group was particularly prominent in Germany and while based on the *Communist Manifesto;* it did not go beyond public agitation demanding cooperative work shops supported by state credit.

Followers of Pierre Joseph Proudhon (1809-1865), French publicist and political economist, the leading exponent of petty-bourgeoisie socialism, also attended the conference. The Anarchists, led by Michael Bakunin, attended, as did the Marxians. The First International was made up of a diversity of revolutionary views.

The goal of the conference was to establish international proletariat solidarity, permitting the labor movement of one country to join hands with workers in other countries. The long-range program anticipated that the parties would be ready sometime in the future for revolution.

The First International failed because of internal dissension. The Lassalleians were essentially Utopian Socialists unable to agree with the Marxians. Michael Bakunin, the leader of the Anarchists, was unable to agree with Marx personally, and Marx succeeded in having Bakunin thrown out of the Communist movement altogether. The Franco-Prussian War of 1871 exploded the idea of international solidarity. Workers of France fought the workers of Prussia. This destroyed any hope of international proletariat solidarity. The First International effectively died in 1872, at the close of the Franco-Prussian War.

The Second International (1889, Paris)

It should be noted that by 1889, Marx was dead; he died in 1883 and was buried in Hyde Park, in London. Engels was still living. The Second International was subject to many of the same weaknesses as the First International, in that a great many radical and liberal groups, not only Marxists, were present. The leadership of the conference was taken over by a group of German intellectuals headed by Edward Bernstein, a man who had been close to Karl Marx. Bernstein initiated the idea that Marxism should be revised, developing the slogan "Revisionism and Reform". By this time, working men had been granted certain rights. Karl Marx had said that the working man has no country, but Bernstein claimed, "Now the working man has a country." Workers, according to Bernstein, can peacefully change the governments of their own countries through a succession of reforms, without resorting to violence.

Reform thus became the end and objective of the revolutionary movement. This premise is basically the idea of the Socialist party today. But working toward reform was not satisfactory to the Marxists and leftwingers at the Second International.

SIX

The Bolshevik Take-Over of Russia

7 November 1917

Early Marxist theorists believed that the Communist dictatorship would be established first in the most industrialized countries where the workers were the most exploited and oppressed. These workers would be willing to follow Communist leadership to improve their social standing and working conditions.

Near the end of World War I, after the Russian army had been badly defeated by the German army, and the Czarist government began to lose control over its long suffering Russian people, the Communists had strong revolutionary elements within the Bolshevik party. It seemed apparent to the Bolsheviks that Russia, in its present crisis, was ripe for take-over. The three most dedicated revolutionaries, and the masterminds of the 1917 Bolshevik revolution, were Vladimir I. Lenin, Joseph Stalin and Leon Trotsky. Lenin, born Vladimir Ilyich Ulganov on 22 April 1870, was from Simbersk, a town on the Volga, deep in Russia. Lenin's father was a school inspector and a devout member of the Russian Orthodox Church. Lenin was one of six children. His youth was short lived, however, as Lenin soon became a revolutionary. As with Marx and Engels, atheism was Lenin's first step to communism. At the age of sixteen, Lenin ceased to believe in God, tore the cross from his neck, threw the sacred relic to the ground, and spat upon it. In 1882, when Lenin was seventeen, his elder brother, Alexander, was charged with conspiracy to assassinate the Czar of Russia and hanged, with four companions.

Five years later, Lenin entered Kazan University and became involved in student uprisings. At the age of eighteen, Lenin started reading Karl Marx and was soon expounding Marxist principles. By his twenty-fourth birthday, Lenin had passed the bar examination with honors and was admitted to the bar in St. Petersburg. Lenin was soon to dominate the Russian Marxist movement. In December 1895, Lenin was arrested, imprisoned, and exiled to Siberia. Five years later, he was released and fled from Russia more ardent than ever for revolution.

For the next seventeen years, Lenin and his wife, Nadezhda, lived in exile in Western Europe, going from city to city, often under aliases, and Lenin was constantly writing, debating, and expounding his revolutionary principles for the overthrow of Russia.

Stalin was born on 21 December 1879 in Gori, Georgia, in the Caucasus region of Russia. He was expelled from the theological seminary at Tiflis in 1899. He engaged in revolutionary activities in Russia from 1902 to 1917, and was arrested and exiled a number of times.

Trotsky, born Leiba Davidovich Bronstein, in Russia in 1879, was an ardent advocate of the Social Democratic party and an able orator from youth. In 1900 he was banished from Russia for participating in the revolutionary labor movement. Before the outbreak of World War I, Trotsky traveled all over Europe, and in 1917 he returned to Petrograd (Leningrad) and became minister for foreign affairs. Later he was head of the Russian army and navy.

In March 1917, revolution erupted in Russia. The German army had defeated the Russian troops. The czar's government was tottering and a liberal regime, later headed by Alexander Kerensky, assumed control. Czar Nicholas II was forced to abdicate. This was the signal for Russian Bolsheviks and other revolutionaries to return to Petrograd. Lenin came from Switzerland, aided by the German High Command, transported across

Germany in a sealed boxcar. Lenin promised that he could bring Russia out of the war. Trotsky arrived from New York City, and brought with him over a hundred dedicated followers. Stalin came out of Siberian exile.

Lenin plotted against Kerensky, eagerly awaiting the moment he could overthrow the new provisional government. He was desperately building up and training his Bolshevik party. He created dissension in the armed forces. He refused to cooperate with the government.

In the fall of 1917, the Bolsheviks seized power in the "October Revolution." Lenin became the dictator of all Russia. On the Western calendar later adopted by the Soviets, the date for the successful revolution was 7 November 1917. The Bolsheviks immediately instituted a terroristic "dictatorship of the proletariat." Czar Nicholas II and members of his family were brutally executed by the Bolsheviks and their bodies were secretly buried. Although the Bolsheviks claim that they defeated the despised Romanov Dynasty of the czars, they actually overthrew the provisional government of Kerensky, which might have ushered into Russia a democratic form of government. Lenin baptized his dictatorship in blood and his ruthlessness shocked the world. The secret police, then known as the CHEKA, instituted a reign of terror; people were slaughtered. A search for "enemies" rocked the country. *Pravda,* the Bolshevik party newspaper, urged drastic measures.

It took Lenin and his co-revolutionaries only sixteen months to sufficiently subdue Russia and start putting into motion Lenin's plans for a world revolution. Lenin's aim was the creation of a Communist world with Lenin and his Communist Party of the Soviet Union (CPSU) as supreme dictator of a Communist world. Lenin convened the Third International world congress to be held in Moscow 2-6 March 1919. The First and Second Internationals had failed and Lenin wanted to make sure his "Communist International" would succeed.

SEVEN

The Communist International

Lenin 1919-1924

The Third International Conference was re-named the Communist International (Comintern) at the First World Congress of the Communist International in Moscow, 2-6 March 1919. Lenin invited representatives from radical revolutionary parties from all over the world. Lenin arranged to issue a manifesto reinstating the idea of violent overthrow of governments into the Communist program, and he rejected entirely the "reform" program of the Second International.

A second Communist International was held the next year and Lenin laid down the thesis and statutes of the Third Communist International. The twenty-one points of the Communist International were adopted in 1920. These twenty-one points made clear the doctrine of international discipline and emphasized the position of the Soviet Union as leader of international communism. The full text of the twenty-one points can be found in the appendix. In part, the points included:

> Every party that desires to belong to the Communist International must carry on systematic and persistent Communist work in the trade unions, in workers' and industrial councils, in the co-operative societies, and in other mass organizations. Within these organizations it is necessary to create Communist groups, which, by means of practical and stubborn work, must win over the trade unions, etc., for the cause of communism. These Commu-

nist groups should be completely subordinate to the party as a whole.

Every party that desires to belong to the Communist International must give every possible support to the Soviet Republics in their struggle against all counterrevolutionary forces. The Communist parties should carry on a precise and definite propaganda to include the workers to refuse to transport munitions of war intended for enemies of the Soviet Republics, carry on legal or illegal propaganda among the troops which are sent to crush the workers' republics, etc.

In connection with all this, all parties desiring to join the Communist International must change their names. Every party that desires to join the Communist International must bear the names: Communist Party of such-and-such country (Section of the Third Communist International). This question as to name is not merely a formal one, but a political one of great importance. The communist International has declared a decisive war against the entire bourgeoisie world and all the yellow, Social-Democratic parties. Every rank-and-file worker must clearly understand the difference between the Communist parties and the old official Social-Democratic or Socialist parties which have betrayed the cause of the working class.

Members of the party who reject the conditions and thesis of the Communist International on principle must be expelled from the party. This applies also to the delegates to the special party congresses.

The Bolshevik party of Russia became the Communist Party of the Soviet Union (CPSU) at the Third World Congress of the Communist International in Moscow in 1921. A Fourth World Congress of the Communist International was held in Moscow in 1922. Lenin remained the dictator of the Soviet Union until his death in January 1924.

After Lenin's death, both Stalin and Trotsky, leaders in the Bolshevik Revolution, strived to take Lenin's place. Many believed that Lenin actually preferred Trotsky but was too weak at the time of his death to push for the transfer of power. Stalin won out, and became the leader of the Soviet Union; Trotsky opposed him. In 1927, Trotsky was "censured" by the government and in 1929, was expelled and exiled. Five years later, Trotsky was charged with instigating treason and assassinations of high Soviet leaders, and many of his followers in Russia were arrested and shot. By 1937, Trotsky was living in Mexico where he continued writing and political activities. On 21 August 1940, a Stalinist agent, Frank Jacson, who had penetrated the Trotsky security forces, assassinated Trotsky by taking an axe to his skull. The Trotskyite movement continued after Trotsky's death but never again reached the level of its earlier influence.

On 3 September 1938, thirty delegates from eleven different countries met together in Switzerland and founded the Fourth International built on Marxism-Leninism as interpreted by Leon Trotsky. World revolution and the establishment of the dictatorship of the proletariat was to proceed in every country of the world simultaneously, according to this protocol. Stalin had taken the Marxist-Leninist revisionist position to make communism work in the Soviet Union and, by example and strength, to show the rest of the world that communism was the better form of government, leading to eventual world-wide socialism.

EIGHT

Joseph Stalin Wins Soviet Power Struggle

Prior to Lenin's death in 1924, maneuvering had begun among the leading Bolsheviks for the position of supreme power in the Soviet Union. Lenin's health had begun to fail in 1921, and he had been forced to curtail his activities. A ruling triumvirate, consisting of Joseph Stalin, general secretary of the party, Grigori Zinoviev, head of the Petrograd party organization and chief of the Third (Communist) International, and Leo Kamenev, head of the Moscow Soviet took over the reins of party leadership. Stalin, Zinoviev, and Kamenev had joined forces against Lenin's heir-apparent, Trotsky.

Stalin's role as general secretary of the CPSU placed him in a most advantageous position in the struggle for power which was to ensue until 1929. Stalin had grown too powerful to be stopped by a dying Lenin. Despite Lenin's warning about Stalin, the triumvirate continued to direct Soviet policies after his death, with Stalin later gaining the upper hand because of his party position. He skillfully used the power of his position to eliminate his rivals one by one.

By 1925, Stalin had succeeded in removing Trotsky from his position as commissar of war. In October 1926, Zinoviev was removed as chairman of the Comintern, and Trotsky and Kamenev were removed from their positions on the Politburo. In 1927, both Trotsky and Zinoviev were expelled from the Central Committee and expelled from the party. A month later, Kamenev also was expelled.

Stalin, as the revolutionary leader, became the interpreter of Marxism-Leninism. Under his rule, the state, which Marx had visualized as "withering away," became even stronger. The army, navy, secret police, and all political structures of the state grew increasingly powerful and entrenched. Slave labor camps multiplied. Soviet society became ironclad, more rigid than under the most autocratic Czar. Stalin carried to the extreme Lenin's concepts of the party as a fanatical, disciplined group. To Stalin, the party was not only a tool with which to seize and maintain power, but also a method of liquidating all political opposition and indoctrinating the masses to the Communist way of life.

After Lenin's death in 1924, Stalin called a Fifth World Congress, but waited until 1928 to call for a Sixth World Congress.

The "Program of the Communist International," with its Constitution, was adopted at the forty-sixth session of the Sixth World Congress of the Communist International on 1 September 1928. A ninety-four-page pamphlet, "The Program of the Communist International," was published by the Workers Library Publishers, Inc. in New York City in December of 1929. The first paragraph clearly states, "The ultimate aim of the Communist International is to replace world capitalist economy by a world system of communism." On page thirty-six, the pamphlet notes

> The conquest of power by the proletariat does not mean peacefully *capturing* the ready-made bourgeois state machinery by means of a parliamentary majority. ... The conquest of power by the proletariat is the violent overthrow of bourgeois power, the destruction of the capitalist state apparatus (bourgeois armies, police, bureaucratic hierarchy, the judiciary, parliaments, etc.), and substituting in its place new organs of proletarian power, to serve primarily as instruments for suppression of the exploiters.

On page seventy-six, under the heading "The Fundamental tasks of Communist Strategy and Tactics," the following statement is set forth:

> The successful struggle of the Communist International for the dictatorship of the proletariat presupposes the existence in every country of a compact Communist Party, hardened in the struggle, disciplined, centralized, closely linked up with the masses.... Despite the bloody terror of the bourgeoisie, the communists fight with courage and devotion on all sectors of the International class front, in the firm conviction that the victory of the proletariat is inevitable and cannot be averted.

The Communists, as late as 1928, were making it positively clear that world conquest was their main aim and purpose.

Stalin waited until 1935 to call for the Seventh and last World Congress of the Communist International. In August 1939, the Soviet Union signed the nonaggression pact with Nazi Germany, which freed Germany to attack Poland in September 1939. Stalin seized the opportunity to take over Eastern Poland as Hitler was taking over Western Poland. Stalin attacked Finland in November 1939 and took over the Baltic states of Lithuania, Latvia, and Estonia in July 1940.

In June 1941, three million German and Axis troops in a surprise attack invaded the Soviet Union, marching through the Ukraine to the Caucasus and through "white Russia" and the Baltic Republics to Moscow and Leningrad. This act was in blatant violation of the nonaggression pact. The Soviet Union was now involved in a life-and-death struggle with Hitler, and the Soviet plan for world conquest had to be postponed.

In June 1943, Stalin formally dissolved the Communist International organization, mainly as a goodwill gesture to the Free World, in order to obtain more military and lend lease materials to aid the Soviet Union in its death struggle with Hitler. As soon as World War II was over, and the Soviet Union was no longer in danger of defeat, Stalin began again to work for a reorganization of the international Communist movement with the Soviet Party at the helm.

In September 1947, Stalin and the leaders of the Soviet Communist party were instrumental in the formation of a new international Communist organization called the "Communist Information Bureau" (Cominform). This organization was in existence from 1947 to 1956. To disguise Soviet control, Cominform headquarters were set up in Belgrade, and later moved to Bucharest. Cominform's official newspaper was called *For a Lasting Peace for a Peoples' Democracy* and was read by members of Communist parties throughout the world. Cominform represented the international Communist line directed by the Soviet leaders.

Stalin died in 1953, and was succeeded by Georgi M. Malenkov (1953-1955). Nikolai Bulganin succeeded Malenkov from 1955 to 1956. Nikita Khrushchev then took over from 1956 to 1964.

In 1956, Khrushchev dissolved the Cominform in an effort to bring Tito of Yugoslavia back into the pro-Soviet Bloc. In 1958, Soviet leaders established a new international Communist monthly journal called the *World Marxist Review,* headquartered in Prague, Czechoslovakia. This journal represented the international Communist position as advocated by the Soviet leadership. Published in thirty-three countries and twenty-five languages, the journal was read in 137 countries.

NINE

Soviet International Conferences

1957-1981

Soviet leaders began to sorely miss the tight control they held over the International Communist Movement before 1956. They decided it was finally time to bring delegates from various Communist parties around the world to an international conference held in Moscow.

Representatives of sixty-five Communist and Workers Parties attended the fortieth anniversary celebration of the Bolshevik Revolution held in Moscow on 7 November 1957. They were invited by Soviet leaders to attend a special conference following the celebration. At this conference, leaders were asked to sign a *Peace Manifesto*.

A paragraph of this lengthy *Peace Manifesto* provides a taste of its contents:

> We, the communists, have devoted our lives to the cause of socialism. We, the communists, are firmly convinced that this noble cause will triumph. And it is because we believe in the triumph of our ideas, the ideas of Marx and Lenin, the ideas of proletarian internationalism, that we want peace and are working for peace. War is our enemy.

By this time, thirteen Communist and Workers Parties had taken over control of their countries. These countries included Albania, taken over by Albanian Party of Labor in 1944; Bulgaria, taken over by Bulgarian Communist Party in 1944; China, taken over by the People's Communist Party of China in 1949; the Republic of Czechoslovakia, taken over by Communist Party of

Czechoslovakia in 1948; East Germany, taken over by Socialist Unity Party of Germany, in 1945; Hungary, taken over by Hungarian Socialist Workers' Party in 1944; North Korea, taken over by Korean Party of Labor in 1945; Mongolia, taken over by Mongolian People's Revolutionary Party in 1945; Republic of Poland, taken over by Polish United Workers' Party in 1945; Rumania, taken over by Rumanian Workers' Party in 1947; Russia, taken over by Communist Party of the Soviet Union in 1917; North Vietnam, taken over by Vietnamese Working People's Party in 1954; and Yugoslavia, taken over by League of Communists of Yugoslavia in 1945.

All of the above ruling parties, with the exception of Yugoslavia's, were invited to a special Communist and Workers Parties meeting in Moscow. The representatives of these twelve ruling parties signed a fifteen-page "Declaration". Yugoslavia was not included because the Soviet leaders felt that Yugoslavian representatives would not sign because Tito was becoming too independent. The "Declaration" ended with the following paragraph:

> The participants in the meeting unanimously express their firm confidence that, by closing their ranks and thereby rallying the working class and the peoples of all countries, the Communist and Workers Parties will surmount all obstacles in their onward movement and accelerate further big victories for the cause of peace, democracy and socialism.

In November 1960, representatives of eighty Communist parties met in Moscow and unanimously adopted and issued a lengthy statement which paid lip-service to the unity of the Communist countries, under the leadership of the Soviet Union, and reiterated the determination of the world Communist movement to achieve the goal of world domination. In this declaration, the United States was singled out as the main enemy of communism. The Sino-Soviet rift became evident shortly after this 1960 conference.

In June 1969, another world conference was held in Moscow, lasting thirteen days and held behind closed doors. This conference was attended by representatives of seventy-five Communist parties. At this conference a document was adopted that called for unity against imperialism. The document also stated that the defense of socialism is the international duty of all Communists. Soviet leaders used this argument to justify the invasion of Czechoslovakia. Soviet leaders were still able to exert considerable control as late as June 1969, as this conference showed.

Following the 1969 conference in Moscow, most Communists continued to manifest their loyalty to the Soviet Communist party. Leaders of some of the other parties occasionally began to show some independence whenever efforts of the Soviet leaders threatened the domestic image of the Communist party.

In the spring of 1971, the twenty-fourth Soviet Party Congress was held in Moscow. In addition to the many international and regional conferences and party congresses, Soviet leaders used bilateral contacts to keep Communists in line. The Soviets, by the carrot and stick approach, provided or took away large subsidies to various Communist parties around the world. Since many Communist parties were dependent on Soviet generosity, and party leaders were given free trips to the Soviet Union for health or vacation reasons, the Soviets were able to ensure continued loyalty of all to the Soviet Communist party. Certain Soviet officials in diplomatic or other status carried out covert contacts with party leaders abroad, and many Soviet diplomats were expelled after being caught in the acts of advising and subsidizing local Communist groups in their long-range plan to overthrow their governments. In 1972, there were 1,154 Soviet Bloc officials in the United States. A large percentage of these officials had intelligence assignments.

In mid-October 1974, delegates from thirty Communist parties met in Warsaw, Poland at the request of the Soviet leaders. Once again, the Soviet leaders tried to pave the way for a Communist super-summit at which they would see the Chinese Communist party declared responsible for the continuing feud between the Soviet Union and China.

Representatives of twenty-eight European Communist parties finally held a special summit meeting in East Berlin in the summer of 1976. This was the meeting sought by Moscow, but it failed to give the Soviet leadership a monolithic Communist movement with the Soviets in tight control. There was no doubt that Moscow had to accept substantial compromises on key ideological points in the twenty months of bargaining before the East Berlin conference. Brezhnev, the Russian dictator, made it clear to all the Communist leaders that

> Our Parties work in different conditions and deal with different problems adapting their tactics and strategy to the concrete situations in their country. But all of us are participants in one single struggle, we all move in one direction and we are all united by a common noble and ultimate goal.

When the twenty-sixth Soviet Party Congress opened in Moscow in 1981, it was attended by 5,000 Soviet Party members and individuals from nearly 100 foreign Communist delegations. Italy, Spain, France, China, and Albania did not send delegates. In a brief speech, the ailing Brezhnev predicted victory for world revolution and stressed a commitment to détente.

TEN

Ideological Dispute

As early as 1956, Khrushchev reported that the Soviet Union stood firmly for the principles of peaceful coexistence, that wars were not fatalistically inevitable and the transition to socialism could take many forms, including peaceful means, in various countries. Khrushchev's position was more or less reaffirmed by the "Joint Declaration" signed by representatives of twelve communist and workers' parties in 1957. It was again reaffirmed in the "Peace Manifesto."

The Chinese Communist party signed these documents, but word began to reach the Soviet Union that the Chinese party was not in accord with the principles of peaceful coexistence and was hinting that Khrushchev's position was a revision of Marxist-Leninist principles calling for continuous revolutionary action until the entire world was Communist.

On 22 April 1960, at a meeting of the Central Committee of the Chinese Party in Peking commemorating the 90th anniversary of the birth of Lenin, a lengthy speech bitterly assailing unnamed revisionists for not following the true Leninist revolutionary spirit was delivered and then published in a book entitled *Long Live Leninism*. This book, distributed in the United States, clearly showed that the Chinese communists were taking a "hard line" in opposition to Khrushchev's peaceful coexistence position.

This ideological dispute broke out into the open at the Third Congress of the Rumanian Workers' Party in Bucharest, Rumania, in June 1960. At this Congress,

Khrushchev vigorously defended his position. The Chinese Party was represented by Peng Chen. According to an article in the *New York Times,* observers in Hong Kong interpreted Peng Chen's speech to indicate a reluctance on the part of Peking leaders to enter into open debate with Khrushchev, despite their deep ideological breach. But there appeared to be no retreat from the hard Chinese Communist's line. Following the Third Rumanian Congress, the Chinese Party, however, joined in signing a communiqué in Bucharest, Rumania, which generally supported Khrushchev's position.

Even though the Chinese Communists continued to sign international party agreements supporting Khrushchev's position, they intended to continue to advocate for their own interpretation of the Marxist-Leninist revolutionary principles.

Nikita Khrushchev, in his report to the twentieth Congress of the CPSU in February 1959, indicated:

> The Leninist principles of peaceful coexistence of states with different social systems has always been and remains the general line of our country's foreign policy. It has been alleged that the Soviet Union advances the principles of peaceful coexistence merely out of tactical consideration, considerations of expediency. Yet it is common knowledge that we have always, from the very first years of Soviet power, stood with equal firmness for peaceful coexistence. Hence, it is not a tactical move, but a fundamental principle of Soviet foreign policy.
>
> It is probable that forms of transition to socialism will become more and more diversified. Moreover, the implementation of these forms need not be associated with civil war under all circumstances. Our enemies like to depict us Leninists as advocates of violence always and everywhere. True, we recognize the need for the revolutionary transformation of capitalist society into socialist society. It

is this that distinguishes the revolutionary Marxist from the reform, the opportunists. There is no doubt that in a number of capitalist countries the violent overthrow of the dictatorship of the bourgeoisie and sharp aggravation of class struggle connected with this are inevitable. But the forms of social revolution vary. It is not true that we regard violence and civil war as the only way to remake society.

In the countries where capitalism is still strong and has a huge military and police apparatus at its disposal, the reactionary forces will of course inevitably offer serious resistance. There the transition to socialism will be attended by a sharp class, revolutionary struggle.

The full text of the Khrushchev report was published in the March 1956 issue of *Political Affairs,* the monthly theoretical organ of the CP, USA.

A report was delivered by Lu Ting-Yi at a meeting held by the Central Committee of the Communist Party of China in Peking, on 22 April 1960. Lu Ting-Yi was probably a member of the Central Committee, alternate member of the Political Bureau and Director of the Propaganda Department of the Communist party of China. While Lu never directly attacked the Soviet Union in his speech, he made inferences about deviations from the tenets of Lenin which apparently refer to the position of the Soviet Union:

The Marxist-Leninists and the modern revisionists, starting from fundamentally different stands and view-points, draw fundamentally different conclusions on this situation. The Marxist-Leninists regard this as an unprecedentedly favorable new epoch for the proletarian revolution in the colonies and semi-colonies. The forces of peace have greatly grown up, and there is already a practical possibility of preventing war. The people of the whole world must further intensify the struggle against imperialism, promote the development of revolution, and defend world peace. The modern revisionists, on the other hand, regard this as a "new epoch" in which the proletarian revolution in various countries and the national revolution in the colonies and semi-colonies disappear from the world agenda. They think that imperialism will step down from the stage of history of its own accord, without a revolution; and that a lasting peace will come of itself, without our waging of anti-imperialist struggles. Thus, whether we should carry out revolution and whether we should oppose imperialism have become the fundamental differences between the Marxist-Leninists and the modern revisionists.

The main arguments of the modern revisionists in revising, emasculating and betraying revolutionary Marxism-Leninism are that under the historical conditions of what they call the "new epoch," Lenin's analysis of imperialism has become "outmoded," that imperialism has "changed" its nature and that imperialism has "renounced" its policies of war and aggression.

The Chinese Communist party claims to be the true Marxist-Leninist Communist party and charges that the Soviet Communist party has revised Marxist-Leninist principles and thereby become soft in the battles against imperialism and capitalism.

ELEVEN

World Strength of the Communist Party Organizations

1973

By 1973, the international Communist movement had increased its membership to ninety-six Communist parties. Fourteen of these parties had complete control over their countries.

Pro-Chinese countries included Albania, with 87,000 Communists, and the People's Republic of China, with 17 million Communists. Soviet-style Communists included Bulgaria (700,000 Communists), Cuba (125,000 Communists), Czechoslovakia (1.2 million Communists), East Germany (1.9 million Communists), Hungary (724,000 Communists), North Korea (1.6 million Communists), Poland (2.2 million Communists), and the USSR (14.7 million Communists). Independent Communist countries were North Korea (1.6 million Communists), Romania (2.2 million Communists), North Vietnam (1.1 million Communists) and Yugoslavia (1.025 million Communists). It is clear that by 1973 the Soviet Union had lost complete control of the international Communist movement. The total membership of the world's ninety-six Communist parties was estimated to be 47.7 million members, an increase of half a million from two years earlier.

By 1973, China had been admitted to the United Nations, and President Nixon had visited China, thereby allowing the People's Republic of China to emerge from international political isolation. The Soviet Union and China continued to eye each other warily throughout

1972, effectively undercutting the long-held Soviet claim that relations among Communist countries were free from friction. Of the eighty-two non-ruling Communist parties, thirty-nine were proscribed in their activities and many countries would not tolerate open Communist activities. There were, however, a number of important countries where the Communist party was making strong headway in effort to take over the country either by force or by parliamentary procedures. In 1973, the Communist party of Italy (PSI) had an estimated membership of 1.5 million, the largest Communist party in the Free World. In the May 1968 elections, the PSI won 26.9% of the 8,555,477 votes cast. The party leadership won 177 seats in the Chamber of Deputies: 28% of the seats. The PSI had control over the country's largest trade union, the three-million strong Italian General Confederation of Labor (CGIL), and the largest cooperative organization, the National League of Cooperatives, with a claimed membership of some 3.5 million, worth hundreds of millions of U.S. dollars.

In France, the Communist Party of France (PCF) had an estimated membership of 295,000. The party itself, at the time, claimed 400,000 members. In the June 1968 elections, the PCF won over 4.4 million votes, 20.03%. The PCF took control of thirty-four seats in the National Assembly (14%). France's largest trade union federation, the Confederation General du Travail (CGT), was controlled by the PCF.

In 1968, the PCF had issued a manifesto which declared that a "socialist democracy," as implemented by the Communists, would create conditions for observance of constitutional rights, such as freedom of expression, thought, and association, better than a bourgeois society. The manifesto also promised to protect minority rights in a socialist France. In October 1971, the PCF issued a 200 page program for a Democratic Government of Popular Union, in which the party presented itself as a responsible partner in a future government, but glossed over the question of whether it would ever allow the transition to communism, once started, to be halted or reversed.

In Finland, the Communist Party of Finland (SKP) had an estimated membership of 47,000 members. SKP was composed of two parties within the group: a liberal majority and a small Stalinist faction. In the March, 1970 elections, the Communist front won 420,572 votes (16.6%) and thirty-six seats in the 200-member parliament. In the January 1972 election, the Communist front increased its seats in parliament to thirty-seven.

The Communist Party of Japan (JPC) had an estimated membership of 300,000 members. In the December 1969 election the JPC won 6.8% of the votes. By 1971, the Communist influence increased to 7% of votes.

Of the ninety-six Communist parties in the world, sixty-nine were pro-Soviet in 1973. Although there may have been some small elements within these parties that would have preferred to adopt a pro-Chinese, neutral, or independent posture, Soviet leaders felt that they could still count on these sixty-nine parties to remain loyal to the Soviet Union as the leader of the international Communist movement. Soviet leaders began to take every step possible to utilize the international Communist movement to further their own imperialist ambitions of conquering the world. The continuing build-up of offensive weapons in Soviet arsenals demonstrated that world Communist control remained the first priority of the Soviet leadership.

TWELVE

Soviet Manual: "Fundamentals of Marxism-Leninism"

Marx and Engels were the formulators of communism. Lenin was the developer and Stalin was the torchbearer of Marxism-Leninism. These four key Communists were prodigious writers. *Das Kapital* (Capital) is undoubtedly Marx's best known and most important work. It is in three volumes: "Capitalist Production" (1867), "Capitalist Circulation" (1885), and "Capitalist Production as a Whole" (1894). The final two volumes were completed by Engels after Marx's death. Marx also wrote *The Civil War in France* (n.d.), *The Poverty of Philosophy* (1847), *Critique of Political Economy* (1859), *Value, Price and Profit* (1865), and *Critique of the Gotha Programme* (1875). In his writing, Marx develops his idea of the dictatorship of the proletariat and the "withering away" of the state. Marx was also a prolific letter writer, corresponding with many revolutionaries in England and abroad. *The Selected Correspondence of Karl Marx and Friedrich Engels (1846-1895)* shows how the intimate collaboration of these two men gave birth to the Communist conspiracy.

Engels, like Marx, was a voluminous writer. Some of his better known works are *The Peasant War in Germany* (1850), *Germany: Revolution and Counter-Revolution* (1851-1852), *The Housing Question* (1872), and *Anti-Duhring* (1877-1878). His *Dialectics of Nature*, published posthumously in 1927, is an attempt to discuss science from a Marxist viewpoint.

Marx and Engels often cooperated in writing, and sometimes it is difficult to determine exactly who wrote what. The best known product of their collaboration is the *Communist Manifesto*.

In *What is to be Done* (1902), Lenin outlines the principles to determine the formation of a Leninist-type party. In 1904, in *One Step Forward, Two Steps Back,* Lenin continues his tirade for a disciplined party. *Materialism and Empirio-Criticism* (1909) is a philosophical treatise and represents one of Lenin's major works. In *Imperialism: The Highest Stage of Capitalism* (1917), Lenin develops the thesis that imperialism is the final state of monopoly capitalism. *State and Revolution* (1918), is probably his clearest blueprint for violent revolution. After the Bolshevik revolution, Lenin wrote *Left-Wing Communism, an Infantile Disorder* (1920), a volume telling other Communists how he "did it" in Russia. Lenin's major writings have been published in twelve volumes under the title *V.I. Lenin-Selected Works*.

Stalin was not as prolific a writer as Marx, Engels, and Lenin. Among his outstanding works are *Foundations of Leninism* (1924), and *Marxism and the National Question* (1913), a study of communism and nationality groups. In the former, Stalin attempts to show that Lenin did not merely rediscover and reapply Marxism but also developed it further. Stalin also claimed to be the genius behind the *History of the Communist Party of the Soviet Union (Bolsheviks)* (1938), a "short course" history of the Bolshevik movement in which the various phases of party development were stressed.

A student of Marxism-Leninism no longer has to read all the works of Marx, Engels, Lenin, and Stalin to get a well-rounded picture of the fundamentals of Marxism-Leninism. An 877 page manual, published by the Foreign Languages Publishing House in Moscow in 1961, titled *Fundamentals of Marxism-Leninism* explains it all. On page 633, the following is printed under the heading, "To be a Marxist is to Admit the Need for the Dictatorship of the Proletariats":

> The dictatorship of the proletariat is the central issue of the ideological differences between the Marxists-Leninists and the reformers... He who limits himself to a simple recognition of the class struggle to the recognition of the dictatorship of the proletariat!... That the question of the dictatorship of the proletariat should occupy a social place in Marxism-Leninism is quite understandable; without the seizure of political power, without the dictatorship of the proletariat, there can be no victory for socialism. The Marxist-Leninist theory of the establishment of a society without classes and exploitation would remain wishful thinking if the working class and its Marxist-Leninist parties did not concentrate their efforts on what is most decisive on making full use of their seizure of power to reorganize society along socialist lines.

Marxist-Leninist Communists were ruthless when taking over a country. Aleksandr I. Solzhenitsyn, Russian Nobel Peace Prize winner in 1970, wrote a gruesome, detailed indictment of the Soviet leadership, *The Gulag Archipelago 1918-1956* (1973), that explains it all. It is a story of the slave labor camps, gulags, and prisons of the Soviet Union and the terrible cruelty of followers of Marxism-Leninism, a philosophy which reduces human beings to less than animals. Millions of Russians died horrible, lingering deaths because they opposed Marxist-Leninist doctrines. In the Communist manual, however, the last chapter, "Fundamentals of Marxism-Leninism," extols Marxism-Leninism and speculates about what a wonderful world it will be when communism is universal.

THIRTEEN

Marxism-Leninism = Death and Human Suffering

The bubonic plague of 1347-1350 wiped out two thirds of the population of Europe: 25 million people. Marxism-Leninist communism, the 20th century Red Plague, from 1917 to 1976, wiped out 50 million people.

In 1989, Zbigniew Brzezinski, former Internal Security Advisor to President Carter, wrote *The Grand Failure: The Birth and Death of Communism in the Twentieth Century*. Brzezinski wrote a harrowing account of the slaughter of citizens in Communist countries (half a million per year) an appalling waste of human life.

According to Brzezinski, in the six years of the rule of V.I. Lenin 1917-1924, more than fourteen million people lost their lives. Lenin did not set out to create a new society, but to crush society, making way for the all-seeing, all-knowing, all-powerful states to be "history's ordained instrument." According to Brzezinski, Stalin snuffed out the lives of twenty million of his comrades from 1930-1953. Between 1937 and 1939, Stalin "reformed" his armed forces by executing 40,000 officers. Extermination or lingering death (usually by starvation) was the fate of "entire categories of people": farmers, political opponents, "hostile" ethnic groups, religious leaders and overly-devout followers, whole families. Brzezinski concludes that "indeed had it not been for the Western aid so assiduously sought by Stalin much of the industrial 'progress' under his murderous regime would not have come about."

Among the most horrible mass killings committed secretly by the Soviet Marxist-Leninists was the massacre of 15,000 Polish Army Officers in the Katyn Forest in 1940. The officers had been captured in September 1939 when they retreated in the face of the advancing German Army at the beginning of World War II. The group was engulfed and captured by advancing Soviet forces, which conquered Eastern Poland, in partnership with Adolf Hitler, under the German-Soviet, non-aggression pact. The 15,000 Polish officers were separated and selected for liquidation were anticommunists and those whom the Soviets did not want returning to Poland after the war. During April and May 1940, these 15,000 Polish officers were gagged and dragged singly from their barracks and placed in front of open pits. Each man was reportedly killed by one of three NKVD Soviet officers with a shot in the back of the neck. It required twenty-four days to complete this gruesome massacre. When the mass graves were eventually discovered by the Germans, they were suspected of being graves of the missing Polish officers. The Germans requested the International Red Cross in Geneva, Switzerland, to conduct an investigation to determine the responsibility for the massacre. The International Red Cross declined because it could act only with unanimous agreement of the membership, and Soviet representatives refused. To this day, Soviets have never been brought to justice for this crime against humanity.

Mainland China

In 1957, Mao disarmed his opposition by initiating his "Let a Hundred Flowers Bloom" movement, which encouraged criticism of the party and government. It was an excuse to flush out dissenters. When he had enough victims, he moved in and crushed all those who publicly criticized either the party or the government. In 1958, Mao undertook the "Great Leap Forward" campaign which combined the establishment of rural communes with a crash program of village industrialization. These efforts failed, causing Mao to lose influence to Liu Shao-chi, who became president in 1959. In 1964 China exploded its first atomic (fission) bomb, and in 1967 it tested a hydrogen fusion bomb.

Mao, with the backing of his supporters, including his wife, Chiang Ching, the defense minister, Marshal Lin Piao, his former secretary, Chen Po-ta, and Premier Chou En Lai, began a struggle to regain power. Chou proposed a movement known as the "Cultural Revolution" at the party congress in 1964. The "Cultural Revolution" was a euphemism for massacre, and tens of thousands of people were brutally slain.

The brutality was ugly and primitive, carried out largely by adolescent "soldiers." It was disorganized and arbitrary. The Cultural Revolution became one of the worst blood baths in world history.

What is hardest to believe is that while Mao indulged his maniacal lusts, he was idolized and glorified by many liberal intellectuals in the Western World, just as Lenin and Stalin had been in the Soviet Union before him.

The occasions of Communist bloodletting are innumerable. Slaughter in Cambodia by the Khmer Rouge cost at least 1.5 million lives. The continuing saga of human rights violations in Cuba is familiar to all Americans. Since seizing power in 1959, Fidel Castro has executed tens of thousands.

On 25 June 1950, the Republic of Korea was invaded by over 60,000 North Korean troops preceded by over 100 Russian-built tanks. Cease fire and armistice talks began July 1951 and dragged on with numerous breakdowns until 27 July 1953, when armistice was signed. Over 54,000 lives were lost in the Korean war and over 100,000 people were wounded in the fight against communism.

In Tibet, too, communism equaled murder. Mao's campaign to extirpate Buddhist cultures turned hundreds of thousands of peaceful Tibetans into corpses. In

Vietnam, 1.3 million Vietnamese and 58,000 American lives were lost to the battle against the Communists.

In the words of Heinrich Heine (1747-1856), the German poet, "communism possesses a language which every people can understand—its elements are hunger and death."

According to the April 1996 issue of the *Reader's Digest*, plans are underway in Washington, D.C. for a long overdue memorial to the victims of communism. The plans are to build a museum, which will document the crimes committed by the disciples of Marx and Lenin. the last paragraph of the article reads as follows: "Rarely do we think of them or of the hundred million. We forget how pathologically evil communism has been or why we poured so much blood and treasure into fighting the Cold War. It is to correct that amnesia that the Victims of Communism Memorial Museum will be built."

FOURTEEN

The Break-Up of the Soviet Union: The Gorbachev Connection

Not one of the first nine Soviet leaders who have served the Soviet Union since the 1917 Bolshevik Revolution has ever repudiated, or in any way modified the Soviet goal of world domination. These leaders were Vladimir I. Lenin, 1917-1924, Joseph Stalin, 1927-1953; G.M. Malenkov, 1953-1955, Nikolai Bulganin, 1955-1956; Nikita Khrushchev 1956-1964; Leonid Brezhnev, 1964-1982; Yuri V. Andropov, 1982-1984; Konstantin V. Chernenko, 1984-1985; and Mikhail S. Gorbachev, 1985-1991. The tenth Russian leader is Boris Yeltsin, 1991 to present, who gave up his Communist party membership and tried to abolish the CPSU altogether.

Many thought that Mikhail S. Gorbachev, the ninth Soviet leader would be different when he began to advocate Perestroika (restructuring of the Soviet economy) and Glastnost (openness) when he took over in 1985. However it should have been crystal clear to the world that he was still a dedicated Marxist-Leninist when he delivered his address on 2 November 1987 in celebration of the 70th anniversary of the 1917 Bolshevik revolution.

Gorbachev ended his two hour forty-one minute speech with this ringing declaration: "In October 1917, we parted with the old world rejecting it once and for all. We are moving toward a new world, the world of communism. We shall never turn off that road."

The beginning of the break-up or fragmentation of the Soviet Communist party took place when Yeltsin, who had been urging faster reform, resigned from the Communist party along with other radicals in 1990.

In March 1991, the Soviet people were asked to vote on a referendum on national unity engineered by Gorbachev. The victory for the federal government was tempered by the separate approval in Russia of the creation of a popularly-elected republic presidency. But six republics boycotted the vote. The bitter re-election contest for the Russian presidency between Yeltsin and a Communist loyalist resulted in a major victory for Yeltsin. He took the oath of office as Russia's popularly-elected president on 10 July 1991.

An unsuccessful coup d'etat was attempted on 19 August 1991, orchestrated by a group of eight senior party officials, the State Committee on the State Emergency. Yeltsin was holed up in the Russian Parliament building, and defiantly called for a general strike. On 21 August 1991, the coup committee disbanded, and at least some of its members attempted to flee Moscow. The Soviet Parliament formally reinstated Gorbachev as president. Two days later, Gorbachev resigned from his position as general secretary of the Communist party and recommended that its Central Committee be disbanded. On 29 August 1991, the Parliament approved the suspension of all Communist party activities pending an investigation of its role in the failed coup.

On 12 December 1991, the Russian Parliament ratified Yeltsin's plea to establish a new commonwealth of independent nations open to all former members of the Soviet Union. The new union included the governments of Ukraine and Belarus who, along with Russia, were the three original co-founders of the Soviet Union in 1922. After the end of the Soviet Union, Russia and ten other Soviet Republics joined in a commonwealth of independent states on 21 December 1991.

At the start of 1992, Russia, under Yeltsin, embarked on a series of dramatic economic reforms, including a move to a free-market economy, which led to downturns. A constitutional referendum, held on 12 December 1993, was a victory for Yeltsin, but the parliamentary elections held on the same day saw the rise of extreme nationalism.

Elections for president of Russia were held on 16 June 1996, and Boris Yeltsin received approximately 35% of the vote, with Communist Gennadi Zyuganov second with 32%. Ex-General Lebed was third, with 12% of the vote and ultra-Communist nationalist, Vladimir Zhirinovsky, received 6% of the vote. Following the election, President Boris Yeltsin appointed ex-General Lebed as head of national security for Russia. This strategy helped Yeltsin. In the run-off election, held 3 July 1996, President Yeltsin defeated Communist Gennadi Zyuganov 53.7% to 40.4%. In a brief televised address, Yeltsin said, "Lets go to work. We have one Russia, a vast country, one Russia, one destiny."

But Russia was still deeply divided over the painful, imperfect reforms that marked Yeltsin's first term. The more liberal economic policies and greater personal freedoms seemed a boon to some, but millions of others have seen their living standards plummet. Some Russians recall the Soviet Communist past with nostalgia.

In mid-October 1996, Yeltsin removed ex-General Lebed as Head of National Security, as he felt Lebed was becoming a threat to him. Yeltsin picked Ivan Rybkin, a low key politician, as his new security chief.

The non-Communist world leaders and investors were thrilled with the Communist defeat in the election which seemed to mandate continued reforms in Russia, and barring any unforeseen misadventures, Russia will hopefully continue non-Communist political reforms toward democracy. Then on 5 November 1996, Boris Yeltsin underwent five-vessel coronary bypass surgery in a hospital in Moscow. Following the seven-hour procedure, the doctors indicated that his prognosis was favorable and he was expected to be able to return to full duty as president. His health, however, considers to be an uncertain factor in the future of the nation.

FIFTEEN

Communism vs. Religion

The most basic of all Communist positions about religion is the statement of Marx that religion is the opiate of the people. Communists have always made it clear that communism is the mortal enemy of Christianity, Judaism, Mohammedanism, and other religions.

Khrushchev, head of the Soviet Union from 1956 to 1964, warned,

> Don't think that the communists have changed their minds about religion. We remain the atheists that we have always been; we are doing as much as we can to liberate those people who are still under the spell of this religious opiate.

Lenin declared, "Religion is a kind of spiritual intoxicant, in which the slaves of capital drown their humanity, and blunt their desire for a decent human existence." Lenin believed in expediency: the end justified the means. In other words, a dedicated Communist can commit murder, pillage, destroy, and terrorize and feel proud; lie and feel no compunction; participate in the establishment of the dictatorship of the proletariat and feel justified if he is serving a higher good. Communism has turned all the moral values upside down. In effect, communism became a secular religion with its own roster of gods, its own Messianic zeal, and its own fanatical devotees willing to accept any personal sacrifice that furthers the cause.

The following are eight basic tenets of Marxist-Communism which every American interested in preserving individual freedoms should remember:

1. Nature is all—there is no God,
2. Body is all—there is no soul,
3. All religions are false and harmful—all religions must be destroyed,
4. Proletarian utility constitutes the moral code—all existing moral codes derived from material concepts are false,
5. History is a materialistic process. It is a history of class struggle—it does not reflect the spirit of man,
6. The capitalist state is an instrument of oppression—it must be destroyed,
7. Revolution and revolutionary methods are necessary—the rulers of nations will not surrender peacefully,
8. Only a world-wide Communist social order conforms to the nature of man: meets the needs of life; is adequate. Therefore, only this type of social order should be permitted to exist—all other social orders must be destroyed.

Anyone interested in determining the true facts will discover that the Soviet constitution theoretically guarantees "Freedom of religion." But this is nullified in actual practice by a series of concrete counter-measures "such as appropriation of church property and state control of clergy and religious activities."

The Soviet law during the cold war went further and prohibited any activity on the part of churchmen or church associations aimed at winning converts. While "religious propaganda" either inside or outside a church building was a punishable offense, anti-religious propagandizing was not only permitted but encouraged.

That religion has survived so many years of harassment and persecution in the Soviet Union and other Communist countries is a testimony to the power of faith. Some religions such as the Baptists, Jehovah's Witnesses, and Jewish Believers were seriously involved in religious confrontation activities inside the Soviet Union, and many of their heroic leaders were sent to Soviet labor camps or subjected to various types of inhuman treatment in Soviet insane asylums.

Religious persecution continues in Russia today, with an estimated 10,000 religious prisoners in custody.

Some readers of this book will recall the anti-Communist lectures and writings of a number of outstanding American religious leaders such as the Catholic Arch-Bishop Fulton J. Sheen and Protestant Reverend Billy Graham. Unfortunately, too many of our three hundred thousand church clergy today fail to speak out publicly against atheistic Marxism-Leninism, which represents the most dangerous enemy that religion has ever faced. If clergy continue to fail to speak out, it is time to fear that Marxism-Leninism, which is far from dead, will continue its march toward complete world domination.

It is a fact of history that no atheist, Marxist-Leninist state has ever tolerated full religious rights or human rights. Marxist-Leninist philosophy has a most unique ally with atheistic and internationalist orientation. That ally is secular humanism, and it is succeeding in winning over supporters beyond all expectation. Secular humanists are providing more and more influence on popular culture of America. Secular humanism parallels many tenets of Marxism. It has been estimated that there are 10,000 pro-Marxist teachers and professors in American schools, colleges, and universities influencing thousands of students each year into varying degrees of sympathy for Marxist and socialist doctrines. These students, after graduation, may move into positions in government, industry, communications media, foundations, and key activist organizations. They may be an expanded force of influence calling for change in America, from our "Free Enterprise System" of government to one based on some form of socialism. Secular humanists also pose an increasing threat to democracy.

SIXTEEN

Communism in the United States
1919-1929

The successful 1917 Bolshevik revolution in Russia electrified the radicals and revolutionaries in the U.S. and they began to agitate for early revolutionary action. The U.S. Socialist Party, which had been in existence since 1901, scheduled an emergency convention at the Machinists Hall in Chicago on 30 August 1919. The radical left wing of the Socialist party was thrilled by the October Revolution in Russia and wanted to establish a Communist party in the U.S. The right wing of the Socialist party opposed. The left wing group, however, could not agree on the proper course of action. One faction wanted to use the emergency convention to take over the Socialist party. Another faction wanted to set up a Communist party immediately. The right wing moderates in the Socialist party, expecting trouble, barred the left wing radicals from the Convention Hall.

One group, headed by John Reed and Benjamin Gitlow, who had been refused entrance, retired to another room in the Machinists Hall (later to the Industrial Workers of the World [IWW Hall] and on 31 August 1919 founded the Communist Labor Party of America (CLP).

The principal rival group, together with a number of foreign, language federations, met at Smolny Hall, headquarters of the Russian Federation, 1221 Blue Island Avenue, Chicago. This group criticized the Communist Labor Party as not being truly communistic. The CLP returned the charges and all attempts at reconciliation failed. On 1 September 1919, the rival group formed the

Communist Party of America (CP) Charles Ruthenberg was chosen as Executive Secretary of the CP of America.

Another split off from the Socialist Party was a group from Michigan who was later to form the Proletarian Party.

Not one, but two parties, the CLP and CP, each claiming to be the true representative of communism and bitterly maligning the other, came out of the Chicago turmoil. The CLP set up headquarters in Cleveland and the CP in Chicago. These Communists were a motley group. They varied in extremes from die-hards who were ready to do anything for the "cause," to apolitical crazies attracted by violent language and subversive possibilities. Many believed revolution in the United States was imminent.

A majority of the Communists were foreign born. Many had difficulty speaking English. The history of the Communist party in United States since 1919 is characterized by two main trends: (1) the development of a disciplined party structure, or, in the words of William Z. Foster, "the building of a Leninist Party of a new type;" and (2) the complete and unquestioning subservience of the party to Russia.

Just a few weeks after the founding conventions in 1919, the U.S. government and state authorities initiated action against the Communists. The first test raid, in late 1919, initiated by Attorney General Palmer, was against the Federation of the Union of Russian Workers. It resulted in a relatively small number of deportations. On 2 January 1920, the Palmer raids swept down on suspected radicals in thirty-three cities, with an estimated ten thousand people arrested; many were new immigrants who could hardly speak English and who just happened to be in the wrong place.

As a consequence of these raids, the Communist movement in the U.S. went underground. Communists met in secret hideouts, maintained underground headquarters, and sent messages by couriers. Hidden printing presses poured out propaganda.

Soon after the 1919 founding convention, the Executive Committee of the Communist International (Comintern) sent a letter to the CP and the CLP. Unity must be established "in the shortest possible time," the letter recommended. There must be one unified Communist party in the U.S. Following the Comintern instructions, in May 1920, a unity convention of the Communist Labor party and a faction, led by Ruthenberg, of the Communist party was secretly held in Bridgman, Michigan, resulting in the formation of the United Communist Party of America (UCP). Many members of the Communist party, however, refused to go along and boycotted the new UCP.

Finally, in May 1921, after another year of bickering, the UCP and the remainder of the CP formed the Communist Party of America, Section of the Communist International.

Heeding the Communist International instructions to get out into the open, among the masses, party leaders in December 1921 formed the *Workers Party of America* as the "legal" outlet for the underground Communist Party. The founding convention was held in New York City. Acting as a front for the underground Communists, the Workers Party set up "open" headquarters, issued a "public" paper, and operated in full view. The Communist movement in the United States now had a dual setup: the underground Communist party, affiliated with Moscow and the Workers Party.

Love for the Soviet Union sent American Communists streaming to the Soviet Union, and they came back, full of stories about marvels of this new land. In speeches all over the country, American Communists claimed that Russia was the only "real democracy" on earth. Working people were better off in Russia than in America, they claimed. Many American Communists went to the Soviet Union as representatives of the party to the Comintern, to enroll in a Communist school, and as sight-seers, to view first hand this Communist "paradise."

During the 1920s the American Communists multiplied labor troubles and participated in a number of strikes, such as the textile strikes in Passaic, New Jersey (1926), New Bedford, Massachusetts (1928), and Gastonia, North Carolina (1929). They participated in the coal strike of 1922, the railroad shopmen's strike of 1922, and the New York furriers strike of 1926.

Moreover, the Communists were beginning to extend their activities far beyond the labor field into other fields. Economic problems, race relations, and nationalism among sub-populations in the U.S. drew their attention.

In 1928 and 1929, acting under Comintern instructions, the American Communist party conducted its first big "purges," the mass expulsion of large groups of members. In 1928, James P. Cannon, an old-time Communist leader, was expelled from the party for displaying Trotskyite tendencies. In 1929, Jay Lovestone, executive secretary of the party, and Benjamin Gitlow, a high ranking charter member, were expelled after Stalin gave his blessings to the William Z. Foster-Earl Browder leadership team.

When the party was reconstituted as the Communist Party of the United States of America (CP, USA) in 1929, for the first time there was considerable harmony inside the movement. After James P. Cannon was expelled from the CP, USA, the Cannonites formed a new party: the Socialist Workers party, loyal to Trotsky. The youth group was the Young Socialist Alliance. The Socialist Workers party is still in existence in America today, and its principal newspaper, *The Militant,* is still published.

There are a variety of dedicated Marxist-Leninist Communists throughout the world. There are those who maintained their loyalty to Moscow and the tenets of the Communist International and those who remained loyal to the Fourth International and Leon Trotsky. In addition there are those loyal Marxist-Leninist followers who admire Mao Tse-tung, Che Guevera, Ho Chi Minh, Fidel Castro, and Kim II Sung.

SEVENTEEN

Communist Party, USA

1930-1945

During the Earl Browder leadership, the American Communist party membership grew more than tenfold. In 1930, after the great "purges," the membership stood at 7,500. By 1935, it had jumped to 30,000 and by 1944 membership was at 80,000. The depression years, as well as President Roosevelt's recognition of the Soviet Union in 1933, aided the Communist party in carrying out its agitation and propaganda activity in America.

The Young Communist League, the youth organization of the Communist party, reached a membership of 20,000 by 1938. During this period, the Communist Party, USA (CP USA) reached its zenith of power. In fact, there were more Communists reported in the United States in 1944 than Bolsheviks in Russia at the time of the Bolshevik Revolution in 1917.

In the 1930s, with the beginning of the depression, the CP USA increased its propaganda-agitation. Economic disorder was exploited. The party organized parades, hunger marches, petition campaigns, and mass demonstrations. The party involved itself with vigor in strikes wherever possible, such as the San Francisco general strike of 1934 and the textile and bituminous coal strikes of 1934-1935.

In November 1935, the Congress of Industrial Organization (CIO) was launched. This group provided the Communists with an ideal opportunity to burrow themselves in its members' unions from the very beginning.

A number of CIO unions came under Communist control.

After 1933, Hitler had become the principal fear of Soviet Russia. The Stalinists, fearing German military power, desperately attempted to enlist the support of the nonCommunist world against the Nazis. The Soviet Union joined the League of Nations and became a strong supporter of the "collective security" program aimed at holding Hitler in check. At this time CP USA became more stabilized, improving its agitation and propaganda functions. Disciplinary machinery maintained "unity" and "correctness of views." This was a period of accepting new members, broadening struggles, and strengthening organizational structure.

The pre-war period was the time of the greatest Communist front activity; some of the organizations were nationwide and captured thousands of innocent victims. Literally hundreds of organizations, such as the American Youth Congress, American League Against War and Fascism (later known as the American League for Peace and Democracy), the American Peace Mobilization, and the National Negro Congress came into existence. Many important Americans lent their names as sponsors or sympathizers to Communist causes without checking into the backgrounds of the behind-the-scenes Communists who were in control.

In the late 1930s, the CP USA published a pamphlet, *The Communist Party—A Manual on Organization,* by J. Peters. The CP USA pledge was printed as follows:

> I now take my place in the ranks of the Communist Party, the Party of the working class. I take this solemn oath to give the best that is in me to the service of my class. I pledge myself to spare no effort in uniting the workers in militant struggle against fascism and war. I pledge myself to work unsparingly in the unions, in the shops, among the unemployed, to lead the struggles for the daily needs of the masses. I solemnly pledge to take my

place in the forefront of the struggle for Negro rights, against Jim-Crowism and lynching, against the chauvinist lies of the ruling class. I pledge myself to rally the masses to defend the Soviet Union, the land of victorious Socialism. I pledge myself to remain at all times vigilant and a firm defender of the Leninist line of the Party, the only line that insures the triumph of Soviet Power in the United States.

To be a member of the CP USA, a person had to declare his or her loyalty to the international Communist ideology and agree to submit to the discipline of the party.

The Manual ends with the following paragraph:

> Every Communist must become a leader of the workers. Every Communist must know that the Party has a historical mission to fulfill, that it has the mission of liberating the oppressed exploited masses from the yoke of capitalism, that it has the mission of organizing and leading the masses for the revolutionary overthrow of capitalism, and for the establishment of the new world, a Soviet America.

In 1936, the Comintern advised their affiliated Communist parties throughout the world that the Spanish "Loyalists" needed help in their civil war to overthrow General Franco (and thereby establish a Communist dictatorship in Spain). Communist parties responded, and brigades from several countries entered the Spanish war. Some of the idealistic volunteers at the outset had no real sympathy for the "Loyalist" cause and did not know they were helping to advance the international Communist movement.

The CP USA formed front groups of many types to recruit and collect money, supplies and medical aid. With much fanfare, the Communists sent about 3,000 "volunteers," commonly known as the "Abraham Lincoln Brigade," to aid the Spanish Loyalists. The Communists were provided with fictitious passports, and an elaborate "convoy" system was established, individuals were taken from the United States, usually through France, to Spain. Any tactic was used to gain manpower for the Communist cause. Sadly, at the end of the war in 1939, only about 1,500 of the 3,000 volunteers survived and returned to the United States. Less than a thousand of these veterans entered Communist activities, but those who did greatly strengthened the party as battle-hardened veterans.

The CP USA leadership was shocked to learn in August 1939 that Hitler and Stalin had signed the infamous "non-aggression pact." This pact resulted in the partition of Poland. It allowed the Germans to invade Poland from the west and the Soviets to annex a large slice of eastern Poland. Hitler now turned toward the west, with his "back" secure. World War II was underway.

The CP USA had no alternative but to back Stalin in this deal with Hitler. The CP USA propaganda was turned upside down. Hitler was no longer a Fascist beast, no longer an enemy, but was now a friend and ally of the Soviet Union. The war between Germany and the western Allies was termed an "imperialist" war, and no support was given to the Allies. The Communists opposed lend-lease, the draft, and military production, supported strikes, and circulated antiwar literature. The new slogan was "The Yanks Are Not Coming."

On 22 July 1941, the CP USA leadership was electrified into action when Hitler double-crossed Stalin and, without warning, suddenly attacked the Soviet Union. The Communists began to claim the European conflict was now a "patriotic war," a "people's war." The United States was compelled to give support, war material, money, and manpower. Russia was being overrun and was in imminent danger of defeat. The Communists must now employ anything to help Stalin: lend-lease, a second front. Strikes must be stopped. Relief must be sent to Russia. Moscow must be supported at all costs.

In 1943, Stalin, in order to obtain more support from the United States and the western Allies, decided to publicly dissolve the Comintern. The purpose was to mollify Western fears and distrust of communism. However, the International Department of the Soviet Party, secretly carried on certain Comintern functions.

Earl Browder, general secretary of the CP USA, without discussing the matter with the Soviet leaders, felt that he, too, should try to win more support for the Soviet Union by changing the name of the CP USA to the "Communist Political Association." This new name did not have the same harsh connotation, but under Earl Browder, the Communist Political Association remained the same faithful lackey of Moscow.

In 1945, World War II finally ended. Hitler was defeated. Immediately, Moscow reverted to its former hostile posture and denounced the Allies and claimed full credit for destroying Nazi Germany. Earl Browder, CP USA general secretary was slow in adapting to the new situation. In April 1945, Stalin reportedly arranged for an article to be published in the French Communist journal, *Cahiers du Communisme,* by Jacques Duclos, the secretary of the Communist party of France. Duclos condemned "Browderism" as a policy of "collaboration" with American capitalism in the operation of the Communist Political Association. This, in Communist parlance, was revisionism, opportunism, and a betrayal. Duclos made it clear that a militant attack on capitalism was needed, not cooperation with it.

The Duclos article was the signal for a purge in the CP USA, and it quickly occurred. An emergency convention of the Communist Political Association was called, and by unanimous vote, except for Browder. CP USA was re-established. Browder was suspended from office and later expelled. William Z. Foster became party chairman. After 1945, CP USA continued to support the Soviet Union and maintained its hostility toward capitalist America.

EIGHTEEN

The Decline of the CP USA

1945-1959

With the reconstitution of the CP USA, communism in the U.S. entered into a new period of consolidation and loyalty to the Soviet Union. The party apparatus was tightened and discipline was strengthened. The party security commissions, with almost unlimited powers, tested the loyalty of members and many were expelled. Admittance of new members was increasingly restricted. Party propaganda cried out against American "imperialism" and argued against the Marshall Plan, the Greece-Turkey Aid Program, and the organization of a West European defense organization, which later became known as the North Atlantic Treaty Organization (NATO). William Z. Foster, the pro-Stalin party chairman, began to weld the party into a real Marxist-Leninist party and into an anti-American weapon of the cold war. Foster was the one Communist leader who could do this. In 1932, he wrote a book, *Toward a Soviet America,* in which he looked forward to a civil war to destroy American capitalism.

After completion of my special assignment at FBI headquarters in Washington, D.C. from September 1945 to January 1946, I returned to my work in the New York office of the FBI. Two months later, in March 1946, I received a transfer to FBI headquarters in Washington, D.C. where I was assigned to work in the "Overthrow and Destruction of the Government Unit" headed by an agent supervisor. This unit supervised the special agents in the field investigating subversive organizations hostile to our government. When I arrived, the unit had two file cabinets containing reports on CP USA and Communist front subversive activities which had not yet been reviewed. Within thirty days, I helped clear up this huge back log and devote more investigative attention to Communist and subversive activities.

Several supervisors in the Domestic Intelligence Division of the FBI agreed with me that our government should take more drastic action against this fifth column Communist enemy agitating openly for anarchy. J. Edgar Hoover, director of the FBI, who had considerable knowledge about Communist activities, agreed that more drastic action should be taken. The director authorized three Domestic Intelligence Division supervisors, E. Hugo Winterrowd, Lish Whitson, and Walter J. Yeagley, all specialists on Communist activities, to work on a comprehensive brief proving CP USA to be in violation of the Smith Act of 1940.

I took over as supervisor-in-charge of the Overthrow and Destruction of the Government Unit since Winterrowd, one of the three assigned to work on the brief, was the man I had been assisting.

The principal provisions of the Smith Act statute were:

> Whoever knowingly or willfully advocates, abets, advises, or teaches, the duty, necessity, desirability, or propriety of overthrowing or destroying the government of the United States or the government of any State, Territory, District or Possession thereof, or the government of any political subdivision therein, by force or violence, or by the assassination of any officer of any such government or whoever, with intent to cause the overthrow or destruction of such government, prints, publishes, edits, issues, circulates, sells, distributes, or publicly displays any written or printed matter advocating, advertising, or teaching the duty, necessity, desirability or propriety of overthrowing or de-

stroying any government in the United States by force or violence, or attempts to do so; or Whoever organizes or helps or attempts to organize any society, group, or assembly of persons who teach, advocate, or encourage the overthrow or destruction of any such government by force or violence or becomes or is a member of, or affiliates with, any such society, group or assembly of persons, knowing the purposes thereof—"Shall be fined not more than $10,000 or imprisoned not more than ten years, or both, and shall be ineligible for employment by the United States or any department or agency thereof, for the five years next following his conviction."

The Smith Act of 1940 was revised in 1946 and 1948. The conspiracy section was revised and, as a result, conspiracy to advocate overthrow of the government became punishable only under the general conspiracy laws. Maximum punishment for conspiracy under that section is a $10,000 fine and five years imprisonment; there is no disqualification to hold public office.

Winterrowd, Whitson, and Yeagley did an excellent job preparing the brief, which ran to three large volumes and contained detailed evidence material and identified key witnesses and former key Communists who were willing to testify against the party. The brief was furnished to then-Attorney General Tom C. Clark in early 1948, and he authorized indictments. The twelve members of the national board of the CP USA were indicted and their trial began in early January 1949 under Judge Medina. The trial lasted until October 1949 and was one of the longest trials in American criminal jurisprudence at that time. William Z. Foster, national chairman and member of the national board of the party, was dropped as a defendant due to poor health. The remaining eleven defendants were convicted, each receiving the maximum penalty of a $10,000 fine and five years imprisonment, except for Robert Thompson, who was sentenced to three years imprisonment because of a record of war heroism during World War II.

The convicted members of the national board were Eugene Dennis, general secretary, John B. Williamson, Jacob Stachel, Robert O. Thompson, Benjamin J. Davis Jr., Henry Winston, John Gates, Irving Potash, Gilbert Green, Carl Winter, and Gus Hall. Four of the eleven top party leaders convicted in 1949, who had been free on bond, did not surrender and went into hiding. They were Robert Thompson, party leader in the New York district, Gus Hall, acting general secretary while Eugene Dennis was serving a contempt of Congress conviction, Henry Winston, party organizational secretary, and Gil Green, leader of the Illinois party district. They were all eventually apprehended by the FBI and served their prison sentences.

While the brief against the CP USA was being prepared, I gave my attention to ways of better investigating and reporting on the activities of the CP USA. In January 1948, I wrote a special agent in charge (SAC) letter which was scheduled to go out to each of the 56 SACs in charge of FBI field offices. The letter directed each office to prepare a report on the activities of the CP USA on a quarterly basis, beginning 1 July 1948.

Agents at the New York office, which covered the national headquarters of the CP USA, were instructed to serve as the office of origin on reporting quarterly on the national activities of the group. Each of the thirty FBI field offices covering a district headquarters of the CP USA would serve as the office of origin in quarterly reporting on the district party activities. The auxiliary offices in the district were to furnish advance copies of their reports to the office of origin so that the information could be included in the district report. The New York office was instructed to prepare two quarterly reports, one on District No. 2 (New York State), the other on national party activities.

The reports were to be prepared in a uniform manner. Information on each special commission activity of the CP USA was to begin on a separate page under the appropriate heading (i.e., Funds, Organization, Membership, Education, Trade Union, Women, Negro, Maritime, Press Department, Veterans, Nationalities, Youth Foreign Affairs, etc.). A copy of the reports sent to the FBI headquarters was to be disassembled, and the pages covering a particular topic were to be placed in a special file under that heading. By referring to one file I could then find out about the nationwide activities of the party on any subject.

Before this, no field agents had any instructions on reporting about CP USA activities. An agent could report on CP USA activities whenever there was anything important to report. The reporting also had no uniformity. With the instructions in this SAC letter, uniform reporting by agents in each office on a quarterly basis was assured.

Just before the SAC letter was to go out, I received a telephone call from the chief inspector of the Inspection and Training Division, who told me that he could not approve this SAC letter. His argument was that after each war, history taught him that there would be increased criminal activity as the soldiers returned home, and that he was beginning to take special agents off security-type work and reassign them to criminal-type work. I pointed out that after World War II, the International Communist Movement had taken over a number of countries in Eastern Europe and was threatening countries in other areas of the world. The CP USA was a part of the International Communist Movement and was becoming more brazen in advocating overthrow of the U.S. government. I strongly requested a hearing on the matter before he made his final decision.

The hearing was held before the chief of the Internal Security Section of my unit: Overthrow and Destruction of the Government. The chief inspector repeated his assertion that criminal activity should be the FBI's main concern, and I strongly recommended that my SAC letter go forward. The section chief, Patrick Coyne, a longtime special agent on Communist activities, agreed with me. Coyne told the chief inspector that he felt strongly that my SAC letter should go forward, and that if the chief inspector did not approve, Coyne would turn in his FBI credentials. Coyne was willing to give up his distinguished FBI career, and finally the chief inspector consented that my SAC letter should go out. I remember very vividly that my SAC letter went forward on 22 February 1948. The reports on the CP USA, thereafter, turned out to be a great help in preparing for the prosecutions of more than 100 members of the secondary party leadership in the early 1950s. After 1948, thanks to these reports, I had a better overall knowledge of Communist activities at the FBI than the general secretary of the Communist party himself. We developed informants in all important segments of party and the special agents in the field became much more knowledgeable about Communist activity in all fields.

More that $20 million was funneled to the CP USA from the Soviet Union between 1958 and 1980 according to these two informants who handled the financial arrangements. The CP USA could not have survived without this subsidy from the Soviet Union. This subsidy also assured that CP USA stayed in line with Soviet aims and desires.

On 4 June 1951, the Supreme Court, in a six to two decision (Justices Douglas and Black dissenting), upheld the convictions of the eleven top members of the CP USA. I had the privilege of being at the Supreme Court when the solicitor general of the United States argued the case before the Supreme Court. I remember him pounding the table and exclaiming, "Must we wait until the enemy is actually battering down the gates before we can take action?"

When the Supreme Court upheld the Communist party leaders conviction in 1951, I was assigned to establish a "Smith Act of 1940 Unit" to further prosecute of CP USA leaders. With a team of five supervisors, we proceeded with prosecutions and convictions of 13 CP USA leaders in New York City, 6 leaders in Baltimore, 7 in Honolulu, 15 in Los Angeles, 5 in Pittsburgh, 5 in Seattle, and 6 in Detroit. Other trials were held in St. Louis and Philadelphia, leading to the conviction of five leaders in St. Louis and nine leaders in Philadelphia. Convictions under the Smith Act stopped in December 1957, when the Los Angeles case (United States vs. Yates et. al.), was reversed by the Supreme Court. The Supreme Court, in effect, held that mere advocacy was not enough for conviction, that there must be strong, overt acts accompanying the advocacy. As a result, courts dismissed pending indictments of Communists or reversed convictions on appeal. By the late 1950s, the Smith Act ceased to be an effective weapon against the CP USA.

In 1953, I was reassigned to the Overthrow and Destruction of the Government Unit as supervisor in charge to ferret out the Communists who had gone underground and to stay on top of Communist activities. The prosecution and conviction of more than 100 communist leaders under the Smith Act of 1940 was a disabling blow to the party. Many of its top leaders had been arrested and convicted. Others lived with fear of arrest. The party went underground in the first large-scale operation since the early 1920s. Party offices were closed, top party leaders went into hiding, records were destroyed, courier systems were instituted, and clubs broke up into small units disbanded. Thanks to the FBI, from mid-1951 to mid-1955, the party, in protecting itself, spent energy, time and money that otherwise would have gone into agitation and propaganda.

Events in the Soviet Union determined Communist activities and policy in the United States. The death of

Stalin in 1953 and the advent of Malenkov brought the "Big Smile" policy from the Soviet Union, continued by Bulganin and Khrushchev. The CP USA, weakened and largely immobilized in its underground activities, welcomed the new line. The party, sensing a new "political climate," began to come above ground. Communist leaders quietly reappeared in public, many courier systems were discontinued and most underground hideaways were abandoned. By the spring of 1956, most of the party's underground had been curtailed and even the Communist leaders who had become fugitives from justice began to surrender. The underground strategy had cost the party dearly.

The party now faced severe problems such as internal disorganization and factionalism. Many members left the party. Administrative affairs were in shambles. Records had been destroyed. Party leaders, returning from arduous underground assignment, were often ignored by the new ruling hierarchy. Money was scarce. Footholds in non-Communist organizations and labor unions had largely been lost.

It was Khrushchev who tried to pare down the influence and excesses of the KGB (Soviet Internal Security Agency) after Stalin's death in 1953. In February 1956 Khrushchev bitterly denounced Stalin in a secret speech before the twentieth Congress of the Soviet Communist party, wherein he outlined in great detail the monstrous crimes that Stalin had committed against the Russian people. This speech, obtained by U.S. intelligence agents, was widely published in the American press. This further helped to devastate the CP USA leadership because Stalin was a "saint" to the American Communists. The bloody Soviet intervention of Hungary in 1956 further devastated the party. Leaders of the CP USA couldn't agree on the future policies of the organization.

William Z. Foster, the national chairman of the CP USA, accepted Khrushchev's denunciation of Stalin, but tried to emphasize what "good" Stalin had done for the Communist movement. Foster and his followers were the so-called Stalinists who wanted as few changes as possible in the party organization. Opposing Foster was John Gates, editor of the *Daily Worker,* the principal daily publication of the CP USA. He openly advocated disbanding the party and establishing a political association. Eugene Dennis was the moderate, but he was not sure what the party should do.

In February 1957, the CP USA assembled in its sixteenth National Convention. The convention was dictated by Foster and a few party leaders. Foster and his associates so effectively manipulated the sessions that the same old Stalinist line prevailed. The party retained its name, and the majority of its old, trusted leadership. It reaffirmed its adherence to the basic tenants of Marxism-Leninism, refused to condemn or even take a stand on the Soviet rape of Hungary, and refused to condemn the tyranny and proven anti-Semitism of the Soviet Union. The CP USA did not take a single affirmative step to declare its independence of the Soviet Union and, in fact, the Soviet-controlled press hailed the CP USA for remaining loyal "to the principles of Marxism-Leninism." Belatedly, seeing the handwriting on the Kremlin wall, John Gates, the editor of the *Daily Worker,* resigned from the party in January 1958.

In December 1959, soon after Khrushchev's visit to the United States, the CP USA elected Moscow-trained Gus Hall as its new general secretary at the seventeenth National Convention. Moscow's control over the CP USA was symbolized by Gus Hall, whose parents were charter members of the party. Having joined the party in 1927, Hall went to the Soviet Union in 1931 to attend the Lenin School, where students were trained in the tactics of revolution and civil war, as well as in sabotage and guerrilla warfare. When Gus Hall returned to the United States from the Soviet Union in 1934, he testified that he would "prefer America with a Soviet government." When asked if he was willing to fight to overthrow the U.S. government, he answered, "Absolutely." He said he was willing to take up arms against U.S. authorities "when the time came."

In 1962, a spokesman for the CP USA placed its membership at approximately 10,000. When I retired from the FBI in August 1963, after twenty-three years of service, seventeen at FBI headquarters, I estimated membership in the CP USA to be about 5,600 dues-paying members. The CP USA was part of the International Communist Movement which, from 1919 until 1963, a period of only forty-four years, took over control of countries comprising one-fourth of the land mass of the world and one-third of the world's population. Too many of our political leaders and too many in the media have underestimated the role of the CP USA as a member of the International Communist Movement, whose leaders had the goal of establishing a world Marxist-Leninist government.

NINETEEN

CP USA

1959-1996

Gus Hall was elected general secretary of the CP USA in December 1959, succeeding William Z. Foster. Hall remains the head of the CP USA and is now identified as the national chairman or national chair. Hall is now one of the longest-serving Communist party leaders in the world. He was born Arlo Halberg in 1910 in Minnesota, to an American Communist family. He was educated in the Lenin School in Moscow in the early 1930s, and served as an organizer for the CIO's Steel Workers in the 1930s. Hall was a long-time Communist functionary, primarily in Ohio, before becoming the top party leader.

The CP USA, under the leadership of Hall, was never able to regain its former strength of the 1940s. In fact, beginning in the 1960s, a number of revolutionary organizations representing the "Old Left," and a number of newly-formed organizations known as the "New Left" began to compete with the CP USA for support of individual revolutionaries. The FBI was kept extremely busy during the 1960s because of the increased subversive activity of the many old and new left organizations.

One of the first embodiments of the New Left was Students for a Democratic Society (SDS). The group was known as the Student League for Industrial Democracy until 1960, and was the youth wing of the League for Industrial Democracy (LID), a fierce anti-Communist organization long identified with democratic socialism. The CP USA did not mount a serious challenge to the SDS because it was still reeling from international and internal problems. The Trotskyites did not pose a real problem, either, because, by 1959, the Socialist Workers Party (SWP), the largest of the Trotskyite organizations, was down to fewer than 400 members. The SWP founded the Young Socialist Alliance (YSA) in 1960. The Trotskyites, headed by Max Shachtman, never realized great importance. Shachtman argued that the Soviet Union was not a socialist state, but was a bureaucratic, collectivized State.

Helped by highly publicized support for the Cuban revolution and black nationalist Malcolm X, the SWP and the YSA enjoyed modest growth in the early 1960s. But splits and continuing disagreements caused a group to break away from the SWP and found the Workers World Party (WWP) which soon abandoned Trotskyism and briefly flirted with Maoism. The WWP formed a militant youth group in 1962 which stood far to the left of SDS. This group earned a reputation as one of the most provocative organizations on the left, carrying flags for the Communist-led Vietnamese National Liberation Front at anti-war demonstrations, and participating in a number of violent protests.

Two other groups were formed by ex-members of the SWP: the Sparticist League and the Workers League.

The Progressive Labor Movement (PLM), a colorful Chinese-oriented breakaway from the CP USA, became a recognized problem in the early 1960s. The leaders of this new organization were expelled from the CP USA because they wanted the CP USA to become politically more aggressive and to admit there was no peaceful path to socialism. In 1964, PLM became the Progressive Labor Party (PLP) and gained about 600 members. By 1965, the PLP had grown to 1,400 members and held its first convention. This Communist organization seemed to offer a brand of communism for New York more militant than that offered by the CP USA. One PLP leader, Philip Abbot Luce, editor of its publication, denounced the House Committee on un-American Activities as the "Scum of Congress."

In March 1965, the PLP expelled Luce on charges that he had become an FBI informant. Luce responded by charging that the PLP was storing arms, training its members to conduct armed warfare, and secretly manipulating other organizations. By 1965, the PLP was making attempts to infiltrate the SDS, which had long abandoned its rule banning Communists. The SDS leaders displayed little concern.

The first Communist anti-war demonstration took place on 2 May 1964 in New York City, led by the YSA and PLP. In April 1965, the SDS called for a mass march on Washington, D.C., to protest against the Vietnam War. In the summer of 1965, the National Coordinating Committee to End the War in Vietnam was formed. The largest anti-war group in the nation was New York Fifth Avenue Vietnam Peace Parade Committee, which included a broad united front including the SWP, the CP USA, and the PLP. The SWP and many new leftist organizations demanded immediate withdrawal of American forces from Vietnam.

By 1966, the conflicts between the Communists and Trotskyites deeply divided the leaders of the National Coordinating Committee to End the War in Vietnam. Frustrated by the disarray, in 1966 a group of radicals formed the National Mobilization Committee (NMC). The Black Panther party was also founded. Ironically, by 1969, with most of its leaders under indictment for their role in the riots at the Democratic National Convention in Chicago in 1968, the NMC became ineffective.

By 1967, the SDS boasted hundreds of chapters and tens of thousands of members, but continued factionalism and differing views among the diverse leadership came to a head at its June 1969 conference. The national leadership led a walk-out and expelled all the PLP members for being anti-Communist and reactionary. The SDS was split in two groups and, by 1970, the PLP-SDS side was down to 3,000 members. For a while, remaining members embraced the Weathermen and Black Panther groups. But at the 1969 SDS Convention, the Weathermen proclaimed that the Black Panther party was the vanguard of the revolution. In the summer of 1969, the CP USA and the Black Panther party cooperated to stage a United Front Against Fascism Conference. To the Weathermen, the duty of a revolutionary was to make revolution. Convinced that the United States was on the verge of defeat in Vietnam, the Weathermen planned a "Days of Rage Campaign" in Chicago for 8-11 October 1969. They called on thousands of revolutionary youths to show up and do battle with the police. Only about 600 revolutionaries came, but they did stage a destructive rampage ending with hundreds of arrests. The "Days of Rage" alienated almost all the radical left which denounced the Weathermen's behavior. The Weathermen's use of guerrilla warfare and PLP-SDA rigidity rang the death knell for the SDS. In 1969 campus groups disintegrated when students refused to follow either a rigid Marxism-Leninism or a violent guerrilla warfare approach.

The Weathermen were still undaunted, and at Christmas 1969, 400 gathered at a "War Council" and decided that the Weathermen would go underground. For the next six years the Weathermen, although underground, carried out a series of bombings. They claimed credit for at least two dozen bombings over a six year period. Most of the bombings were directed at police stations, military installations, and corporate headquarters. The most destructive explosion took place in March 1970 at a Greenwich Village townhouse being used as a bomb factory by one of the Weathermen group. Three people, including a Weathermen leader were killed.

In April 1971, a coalition of radical forces cooperating with the CP USA, calling itself the People's Coalition for Peace and Justice, coordinated the largest anti-war demonstration in American history. The increasing scale of American involvement in Vietnam and the growth of such liberal and moderate organizations as the Vietnam

Moratorium reduced the effectiveness of the more radical groups.

As the strength of the New Left waned, some disillusioned members joined the CP USA. Still, as late as the 1970s, CP USA membership remained below 10,000. Party membership has never been the only Communist influence. Hall, noting the shifting political climate in America, decided to run for president in all four elections from 1972 to 1984. Hall won 25,000 to 59,000 votes. In the 1984 election, he received only 35,000 votes, and in the 1988 elections, the CP USA decided to back the Democratic candidate. By 1990, the CP USA concluded that it was best to try to bring about a reconstituted Democratic party. It strongly backed Jesse Jackson and his Rainbow Coalition in an effort to gain strength in the Democratic party and transform its policies and objectives. In a speech on June 1991, Hall accused Gorbachev of endorsing the liquidation of the CP of the Soviet Union, and harshly criticized Gorbachev for surrendering the USSR to capitalism.

For many years, the Soviet Union had subsidized the CP USA with as much as two million dollars per year. It was this support that kept the CP USA alive. The June 1990 issue of *Harper's Magazine* published a letter from Hall to Anatoly Dobrynin, secretary for international relations of the Soviet Communist party, in which Hall pleaded for an extra grant of $2 million in addition to the $2 million already granted. Hall's letter was discovered early in 1992 in Gorbachev's personal files by Russian prosecutors investigating the August 1991 coup attempts. It was reported that two months after the Hall's letter was sent, Hall received $2 million from a KGB courier. Here is the text of Hall's letter:

> Dear Comrade:
>
> I don't like to raise the question of finances, but when the 'wolf' is at the door, one is forced to cry out. Our financial crunch at this moment is the

result of a number of special developments that have been forced on us simultaneously.

First, we have been forced to establish a new print shop outside New York City. This is an expensive operation, but we had no choice. We know that the FBI had a hand in creating this situation.

Also, we went all out in (1986) congressional elections, which in my opinion, paid off very well. However, as I am sure you are aware, no matter how tightly one holds the purse strings, election campaigns are a costly business. Of course, what we spent was peanuts compared with bourgeois candidates: the average campaign expense for a U.S. Senator is now about $20 million. But the fact is, we were influential, and even the deciding factor, in the defeat of some of the extreme Reaganite candidates.

Because of inflation, the cost of everything we do keeps going up. The taxes and upkeep of our headquarters building increased every year. Selling the building, which I have often considered, would be a serious political setback for the Party. The truth is, that in spite of the fact that our Party raises about twice as much money now than at any other time in history, we still face a serious crisis. We have already been forced to cut back in a number of areas.

The cold fact is that we have been able to function in the past years because of the very generous (Soviet) contribution of approximately $2 million per year. In order for us to continue functioning effectively on the present level, that $2 million is needed. But for us to get out of our current special crisis, we have to find an additional $2 million.

I have some idea of the financial demands you comrades must face. And I am sure that everyone believes that his problems are the most important. I can only argue that because our Party works in the decaying heart of imperialism, whatever we do has a worldwide impact. And because of the crisis of the Reagan Presidency, which is deep and chronic now, our Party's work has had, and continues to have, a growing impact on the politics of our country.

Therefore, in the context of the struggle against the U.S. imperialism and the policies of the Reagan Administration, our Party must be seen as an important, even indispensable, factor.

Comradely,

Gus Hall

The CP USA publishes a weekly newspaper called *People's Weekly World,* primarily for agitation, and a monthly theoretical organ called *Political Affairs* primarily for propaganda purposes and to set the party line. The 6 July 1991 issue of the *People's Weekly World* advised that Hall had returned from a four-week visit to Moscow that included high-level meetings and discussions with CPSU leaders and others. The article further advised that Hall had for several years been in the forefront of a call for a meeting of Communist and workers' parties from capitalist countries. Hall reported new interest and new progress in that direction because of his trip.

The 1 September 1992 newsletter of the Christian Anti-Communist Crusade advised that a group of the CP USA leading intellectuals and public figures had dared to protest Hall's dictatorial rule and were expelled from the party. These individuals organized a conference which was held on the campus of the University of California at Berkeley, on 17, 18, and 19 July 1992. The conference was well attended, with over 1,000 registered. The principal purpose of the conference was to open a discussion of the idea of instituting a new party eighteen months after the date of the conference. The 31 July 1993 edition of *People's Weekly World* contains a passionate plea by Hall to ex-members of the party and to fellow travelers to rejoin or join the party and to cooperate in a great Communist advance.

TWENTY

The FBI in the Forefront

J. Edgar Hoover, director of the FBI, understood better than most other government leaders the menace of international communism. While I was in key supervisory positions at FBI headquarters in the fight against communism from 1946 to 1963, I recall Mr. Hoover's efforts to keep the American people informed of the Communist threat. Each year, in his annual testimony before Congress regarding the appropriation of funds for the FBI, Hoover would bring Congress up to date on the latest machinations of the CP USA.

On 9 June 1947, Hoover furnished a lengthy article to *Newsweek* magazine about "How to Fight Communism." This exclusive article was reprinted and given wide circulation. The article ended with the following advice:

> Don't label anyone as a Communist unless you have the facts.
>
> Don't confuse Liberals and Progressives with Communists.
>
> Don't take the law into your own hands. If Communists violate the law, report such facts to your law enforcement agency.
>
> Don't be a party to the violation of the civil rights of anyone.
>
> When this is done, you are playing directly into the hands of the Communists.
>
> Don't let up on the fight against real Fascists, the KKK, and other dangerous groups.

Don't let Communists in your organization or Labor Union out-work, out-vote, our out-number you.

Don't be hoodwinked by Communist propaganda that says one thing but means destruction of the, "American Way of Life."

Expose it with the truth.

Don't give aid and comfort to the Communists cause by joining front organizations, contributing to their campaign.chests or by championing their cause in any shape or form.

Don't let Communists infiltrate into our schools, churches, and moulders of public opinion, the press, radio and screen.

Don't fail to make democracy work with equal opportunity and the fullest enjoyment of every American's right to life, liberty and the pursuit of happiness.

If Joseph McCarthy had heeded Hoover's advice, the word "McCarthyism" would never have been coined

On 1 March 1960, Hoover sent out the following letter to all law enforcement officials which was a reprint of an article in the March 1960 *Law Enforcement Bulletin:*

TO ALL LAW ENFORCEMENT OFFICIALS:

It is an incontestable fact that our country, the symbol of the free world, is the ultimate, priceless goal of international Communism. The leaders of international Communism have vowed to achieve world domination. This cannot be until the Red flag is flown over the United States.

If, for a moment, the grandiose Red plan is scoffed at as being fantastic, consider that one-fourth of the land surface of the world and one-third of the peoples of the earth are now controlled by the world-wide communist bloc.

Certainly, the Communist gains throughout the world are evidence enough that America, if it lowers its guard, may be someday an easy target for the Red threat. The Communist plan is to conquer the United States, if not today, then tomorrow; if not tomorrow, then the next day, next month, next year—there is no timetable, no "Five-Year Plan." This is evident in the machinations of the CP USA, as shown by the analysis of its 17th National Convention published in this Bulletin.

It is indeed appalling that some members of our society continue to deplore and criticize those who stress the Communist danger. What these misguided "authorities" fail to realize is that the CP USA is an integral part of international Communism. As the world-wide menace becomes more powerful, the various Communist Parties assume a more dangerous and sinister role in the countries in which they are entrenched. Public indifference to this threat is tantamount to national suicide.

Lethargy leads only to disaster. The Communists have a savage plan of liquidation for a vanquished America. The blueprint can be found in the words of Mao Tse-tung, Chairman of the Chinese Communist Party, who reportedly said that is was necessary to liquidate 800,000 "enemies" to solidify Communism in China. Another pattern is the plight of countless families in satellite countries who were torn apart and transported to the oblivion of Soviet labor camps.

Under Communist domination in America, the first campaign of liquidation would engulf the lawyers, champions of due process of law; newspapermen, whose ageless fight for freedom of expression would have no place under totalitarianism; law enforcement officers, guardians of individual rights; governmental leaders, local, state, and national; and everyone falling in the so-called "capitalist" category. Occupations and professions which the

Communists term "useless and parasitic" would be abolished—clergymen, wholesalers, jobbers, real estate salesmen-the list for purging is endless. No citizen would escape some form of suffering under a communist regime. One need but to compare his own worth, his own ideals, his own religious beliefs with the atheistic doctrines of Communism to determine his priority on the list of liquidation.

The defense of the cherished freedoms secured and handed down to us by our forefathers is the responsibility of each American. Knowledge of the enemy, alertness to the danger, and everyday patriotism are the brick and mortar with which we can build an impregnable fortress against Communism. Only the intelligent efforts of all Americans can prevent the decay of public apathy laying open our Nation to the Red Menace.

Very truly yours,

John Edgar Hoover

Hoover, over the years, made FBI speakers available to speak knowledgeably about the Communist menace. For many years, I gave a three hour lecture on communism to agents attending the Office of Naval Intelligence (ONI) School at the Pentagon. I was also assigned to give special lectures before the Strategic Intelligence School which trained government employees with "top secret" clearance.

On 2 May 1954, I was privileged to give the keynote address before the annual National Executive Committee of the American Legion in an "off the record" speech on the "Menace of Communism." I was the replacement for Hoover, who could not attend because of a schedule conflict.

Mr. Hoover's 1958 book, *Masters of Deceit*, is one of the most informative books ever published on the subject of communism. Hoover's *A Study of Communism* (1962) is also an excellent book which clearly explains the machinations of communism.

During the Korean War (June 1950-27 July 1953), I was assigned to write daily letters to the president, the attorney general, and the heads of the Naval, Army and Airforce Intelligence Services which set forth important developments in the Communist field. Later, the number of letters grew to ten instead of these five. Also during the Korean War, I was assigned to prepare quarterly monographs on important Communist activities which were sent to each of the countries comprising the North Atlantic Treaty Organization (NATO).

When Hoover died in 1973, one-fourth of the land mass and one-third of the people of the world, in fifty countries, were languishing under totalitarian Marxist-Leninist-Maoist Communism. Hoover's warning about the Communist menace apparently fell on deaf ears because many Americans were lukewarm in the fight against communism. There was no real turning of our top governmental officials against the onslaught of international communism from 1945, until President Ronald Reagan took charge in 1981 and dared to call the Soviet Union an "Evil Empire in 1991." The Soviet Union began changes in earnest and the cold war with the Soviet Union officially ended. Yeltsin, now a non-Communist, became the leader of the Commonwealth of Independent States formerly known as the Soviet Union. But the cold war with the USSR may have been a prologue for our relations with the People's Republic of China, where 1.2 billion people still live under Communist subjugation.

TWENTY-ONE

Franklin Delano Roosevelt Administration

4 March 1933-12 April 1945

President Franklin Roosevelt and his administration gave much aid and comfort to the Soviet Union and Marxist-Leninist communism during the twelve years and two months that he was in office. Although Roosevelt should have been aware of the Communists' drive to establish a "one world Communist dictatorship" and certainly should have known of the millions of Soviet citizens who were murdered or sent to slow death in Soviet gulags (Soviet labor camps) following the Bolshevik revolution in 1917, President Roosevelt apparently closed his eyes and ignored the merciless brutality of communism.

The media were especially kind to Roosevelt from the very beginning of his administration. In 1921, Roosevelt was stricken with polio that permanently crippled him from the waist down. But by indomitable effort, he learned to walk again using leg braces and crutches. The media kept the fact that President Roosevelt was confined to a wheelchair most of the time from the American public. During the fireside chats and other public appearances, he was always shown comfortably seated or standing in such a manner that his disability was not noticeable. When he ran for a fourth term in 1944, during the middle of the war, he was in extremely poor health, which was also kept from the American people. If the voters had really understood the extreme seriousness of Roosevelt's illness, he certainly would not have been re-elected for a fourth term. As a result of his poor health, Roosevelt was endangering the best interests of our nation.

Here is the story of Roosevelt's political mistakes, one after another, that are not mentioned or are lightly glossed over in the biographical literature. One of the early, major decisions made by Roosevelt after taking office in 1933 was to give diplomatic recognition to the Soviet Union, thereby providing it with prestige and credit it needed to save it from the financial collapse. Roosevelt opened Pandora's box, no doubt about it. The world would have been saved much tribulation if the Soviet Union had been allowed to die on the vine as a third class world power. During the Soviet Union's turbulent 1930s, Roosevelt's administration failed to raise strong outcries against Stalin for his rigged purge trials, or for his ruthless suppression of the Soviet people which caused untold deaths, imprisonments and human suffering. In 1939, Roosevelt was advised that Alger Hiss, a key diplomat in the U.S. State Department, was a Soviet spy. Roosevelt refused to take any action against Hiss, or have him investigated by the FBI. The full extent of the damage inflicted on our country by Alger Hiss has never been publicly assessed. It is an unbelievable story.

Alger Hiss, a Harvard University graduate, worked his way up in the U.S. State Department during the 1930s into a top echelon position. Hiss seemed a typical, well-dressed, highly-respected, intelligent, and capable diplomat. On 2 September 1939, a different picture began to secretly unfold when Whittaker Chambers, editor of *Time* magazine (who had been a member of the CP USA from 1924 to 1937) was a special dinner guest at the home of Assistant Secretary of State Adolf Berle. At this dinner, attended by Berle and Isaac Don Levine, a journalist and well known anti-Communist, Chambers revealed the existence of a secret cell of Soviet agents strategically placed in the most sensitive areas of the U.S. government. One of those he named was Alger Hiss.

Chambers asked that Berle bring the matter to the personal attention of Roosevelt. Berle did so, but Roosevelt shrugged the whole matter off and did not advise the FBI.

In 1945, Igor Guezenko, a code clerk working for the Soviet Military Attaché in Ottawa, Canada, took his wife and small child and secret Soviet files on a desperate flight for freedom. He turned over more than 100 documents to the Royal Canadian Mounted Police, which disclosed the outlines of a vast Soviet espionage network. These documents named Alger Hiss as a Soviet spy. During the summer of 1948, the House Committee on Un-American Activities (HCUA) called Whittaker Chambers and others to testify. By this time, Hiss had learned of the possible charges against him and had quietly left his State Department position. In 1947, Hiss had been appointed president of the Carnegie Endowment of International Peace. The public testimony before the HCUA by Chambers naming Alger Hiss a Soviet spy was incriminating. His testimony covered clandestine contacts with Hiss during the 1930s. Hiss vehemently denied all charges. Hiss sued Chambers for calling him a Communist and further charged Chambers with perjury. This suit helped seal Hiss' doom. At the last minute, Chambers, believing he might lose the case, reacted in a cloak and dagger scene, by taking then-Congressman Richard Nixon of the HCUA at night to a pumpkin in Chambers' Maryland garden and from the pumpkin withdrew five rolls of microfilm containing photostat copies of confidential and secret documents stolen by Hiss from the State Department files and given to Chambers to forward to the Soviet Union. A New York Grand Jury, on the verge of indicting Chambers for perjury, reversed itself and brought in an indictment for perjury against Alger Hiss.

The investigation of Alger Hiss by the FBI was a major undertaking. In all, 263 special agents worked on the Hiss investigation in forty-five of the FBI's then fifty-two field divisions. The FBI investigations bore out the full truth of the Chambers' disclosures and led to successful prosecution of Hiss for perjury. Hiss eventually served forty-four months of a five-year sentence for perjury, but escaped more severe punishment under the espionage statutes because the statute of limitations had expired.

Since serving his prison sentence, Hiss has been active going all over the country giving speeches, pleading that he needed vindication for the "malicious" espionage charges against him. At the age of seventy, Hiss had his right to practice law in Massachusetts reinstated. Hiss died on 15 November 1996 at the age of ninety-two.

Allen Weinstein, a liberal history professor, took on the challenge to prove Hiss innocent. He examined 30,000 pages of classified FBI files and thousands of pages of other Department of Justice material, plus oral evidence from over eighty persons. He interviewed Hiss half a dozen times, traveled 125,000 miles, and worked on the project for four years. When his book *Perjury* appeared in 1978, he found that Hiss was guilty as charged.

Alger Hiss' damage to the U.S. has still not been calculated. In August 1939, the Soviet Union signed the nonaggression pact with Nazi Germany, allowing Hitler and the Soviet Union to divide up Eastern Europe on each side of the Curzon line in Poland. Britain and France retaliated by declaring war on Hitler on 1 September 1939. Hitler then double-crossed his ally, Stalin, by suddenly launching a massive invasion of the Soviet Union in June 1941. All the pro-Soviet and pro-Communist organizations and individuals in the United States who had been supporting Stalin and the Soviet Union during the two year nonaggression pact were taken by surprise. They had been calling for peace and noninterference with the Hitler war against Western Europe. No longer was Nazi Germany an ally of the Soviet Union; it was now threatening the very existence of the Soviet Union.

Literally thousands of pro-Soviets and pro-Communists in the United States, who had been active on behalf of the Soviet Union within such Communist front organizations as the American League Against War and Fascism, The American League for Peace and Democracy, and The American Peace Mobilization, changed their positions overnight. The American Peace Mobilization changed its name to the American People's Mobilization and began to call for full support of the Soviet Union against the now-hated Nazi invaders. The cry for support for the Soviet Union became loud and clear from the Communists, including 70,000 members of the CP USA and many pro-Communist front organizations.

The international situation changed drastically when Japan carried out its sneak attack on Pearl Harbor on 7 December 1941, following which Roosevelt declared war on Japan and, later, on Germany and Italy. Now that the United States was in the war against Hitler, pro-Soviet and pro-Communist elements gave full attention in their propaganda efforts to get as much aid as possible for the Soviet Union. Roosevelt lost no time in aiding the Soviet Union by making certain the Soviet Union received maximum aid under the Lend Lease Act of 11 March 1941. More than fourteen billion dollars of lend lease materials were furnished to the Soviet Union during the war years and, under the extension pipeline agreement of 1945, up until 1947. Roosevelt seemed to have little concern about the thousands of merchant marines who lost their lives bringing convoys of Lend Lease materials to Murmansk, USSR.

The lend lease debt has never been repaid, and we have received very little Soviet thanks for our wartime assistance. It probably saved the Soviet Union from defeat at the hands of Hitler, and this assistance allowed the Soviet Union to emerge from the war in better condition than it was in 1940, almost on parity with the United States in plant industrial capacity.

Roosevelt again came to the aid of the Soviet Union in 1943, when information was furnished to him regarding the brutal massacre in Katayn Forest of 15,000 anti-Communist Polish officers who had been captured by the Soviets in 1939. Roosevelt reacted against the disclosure rather than against the Soviets who had committed the atrocity.

From 1943 to 1945, Roosevelt participated, with Churchill and Stalin (whom he affectionately called "Uncle Joe,") in the Teheran Conference. The result of this conference was to fill the political vacuum created in Central Europe and the Balkans with the Communists. This not only determined the military strategy for 1944, but adjusted the political balance of post-war Europe in favor of the Soviet Union. At Teheran, Roosevelt gave up to the Soviet Union, beyond hope of recall, the Baltic States and the territory of Poland east of the Curzon line. It provided support of Tito in Yugoslavia, at the expense of the loyal patriot, General Mihailovic, who would have kept Yugoslavia out of the Soviet Bloc.

Roosevelt participated, again with Churchill and Stalin, this time at the Yalta Conference. Roosevelt was by this time in failing health, and one of his eager assistants at the conference was the State Department official Alger Hiss, who had been identified to the president back in 1939 as a member of the Soviet espionage apparatus. James Byrnes, one of Roosevelt's advisors, and later secretary of state under President Truman, claimed that at Yalta, "More time was spent on Poland than on any other subject."

On the Soviet side of the table were Stalin; the bloody-handed secret policy chief, Beria; Vishinsky, prosecutor of the infamous purge trials; and Molitov, who had arranged the infamous nonaggression pact with Nazi Germany in August 1939. No wonder the United States could not get an even break at this conference, on such an uneven playing field as this. Among the secret deals at Yalta were protocols calling for forced German labor, in contravention of the Geneva convention, reportedly resulting in deaths of at least one million German soldiers in slave labor camps in the Soviet Union, forcible repatriation of 3.7 million Soviet citizens from Western Europe under the code name of "Operation Keelhaul," and allowing the Soviet Union to have three votes in the United Nations.

George N. Crocker, in his book *Roosevelt's Road to Russia,* claimed that, "What followed Yalta was mass expulsion which Churchill himself was impelled to allude to as 'tragedy on a prodigious scale.' " Actually, never in history, even in the worst of pagan times, has there been such a million-fold uprooting of human beings. By the fall of 1945, shocked voices in England claimed that it was the most enormous official atrocity in all the world's history. Roosevelt did not live to see the results of his wrongful political decisions, as he died at Warm Springs, Georgia, in April 1945.

Another indictment of the Roosevelt era was revealed in the book *The Eleventh Hour,* written in 1979 by General Lewis W. Walt, USMC (Ret.). According to General Walt, a National Security Council Memorandum #68 was declassified after twenty-five years of secrecy. This NSC document was based on the analysis and policies advocated by Gorge F. Kennan and first drafted by him in 1945 while he was charge d'affaires at the U.S. Embassy in Moscow with Ambassador Averell Harriman. While replaced by other written policies, the basic philosophy of NSC #68 reportedly continued to dominate the foreign policy of our government up to at least 1979.

NSC #68 in essence, while recognizing the aggressive aims of the Soviet Union, committed us to avoiding a nuclear war, even to the extent of accepting a Soviet first strike. Secondly, it committed us to confining our military actions to limited counteractions. Thirdly, it advocated seeking co-existence in the hope that the Soviet Union would gradually evolve into a more compatible world partner; and fourth, it committed us to a policy of "containment" but of never directly challenging Soviet prestige.

Why didn't the Senate Foreign Relations Committee conduct hearings regarding NSC #68 to determine the part it played in the Korean and Vietnam "police action" conflicts? I believe that such hearings would bring out the fact that Secretary of Defense, Robert S. McNamara drew up his "rules of engagement" for the Vietnam conflict in conformance with NSC #68. These rules were kept secret for years and not revealed until Senator Barry Goldwater placed them in the Congressional Record on 6 June 1975.

Military men who operated under these "rules of engagement" certainly must have known that no other armed force in modern history was ever called upon to fight under such severe restrictions, which actually aided the enemy. U.S. superiority in both air and artillery fire power was deliberately not exploited in North or South Vietnam. The families of the 58,000 men who died and the thousands who were wounded in action deserve to have those responsible for the asinine "rules of engagement," answer for them and, thereby, make sure the United States will never fight in another "police action," but will only fight in a declared war that will be fought to be won.

On 12 April 1985, the fortieth anniversary of the death of Franklin D. Roosevelt, the Soviet news agency, TASS, carried two long stories praising Roosevelt as a "Statesman of world caliber" and "a convinced champion of cooperation with the Soviet Union." Their praise of Roosevelt was well supported by his decisions in their favor.

At Yalta, in Crimea, on the Black Sea, Roosevelt is honored by a street bearing his name, which connects with Lenin Square near the city's harbor. Two rooms are maintained at Livadia Palace at Yalta, where the conference took place; one is a large hall with an immense round table in the center where the American, English, and Soviet delegations met to hammer out the Yalta Agreement. The other is a smaller wood paneled sitting room, known as Roosevelt's Room, where he met with Stalin for private discussion, which resulted in this historic sellout.

TWENTY-TWO

FBI Thwarts the First Clandestine Group of Soviet Atom Spies

Roosevelt probably did more than any other person to assist the Soviet Union in its insatiable goal to establish a worldwide Communist dictatorship. Roosevelt's recognition of the Soviet Union a few months after becoming president in 1933 gave Stalin and his Communist government the shot in the arm it so badly needed. This was at a time when the Soviet Union reportedly was almost bankrupt and ready to fall. If Roosevelt had allowed the Soviet Union to self-destruct, it might have been replaced by a democratic regime, or at least an anti-Communist one. If this had occurred, we might not have had World War II, the Korean Police Action, or the Vietnam conflict. We almost certainly would have been spared the cold war.

But Roosevelt, for some unknown reason, had admiration for Stalin, one of the bloodiest murderers who ever lived. He not only affectionately referred to Stalin as "Uncle Joe," he trusted Stalin blindly. During World War II, Roosevelt insisted on full support for the Soviet Union, and our country poured more than fourteen billion dollars of lend-lease materials into the Soviet Union. Roosevelt reportedly even went so far as to have an accord with Stalin that neither the United States nor the Soviet Union would spy on each other. I regret that Roosevelt did not live long enough to realize that he had been badly duped by Stalin.

The FBI performed a great service to the American people by helping to prevent the Soviet Union from developing the atomic bomb before we did in 1945. Had the Soviet Union been successful first in producing the atomic bomb, I am certain the entire world would now be languishing under Marxist-Leninist Communist dictatorship.

Was there a chance the Soviets could have produced the atomic bomb before we did? They certainly tried. From the early 1940s, the Soviets engaged in an all-out effort to be the first to develop an atomic bomb. Here are some facts the American people should know which I learned first hand as a key security special agent in the New York office of the FBI during 1943-1945.

The United States' efforts to build the bomb got underway in July 1939, when three leading scientists, Leo Szilard, Edward Teller, and Albert Einstein, got together and discussed the development of an atomic bomb. Following the meeting, on 2 August 1939, Einstein wrote his famous letter to Roosevelt suggesting such an effort. Eventually, the U.S. government initiated a crash research program to develop the atomic bomb under the management of the Manhattan Engineer District at several universities and laboratories around the country.

My story begins March 1943. Steve Nelson, a member of the National Committee of the CP USA, an honor graduate of the Lenin Institute of Moscow, and "hero" on the Loyalist side of the Spanish civil war, was one of a number of Americans who played important roles in providing assistance to the Soviet espionage apparatus in its efforts to obtain American atomic bomb secrets. On 29 March 1943, a scientist working at the Radiation Laboratory at Berkeley, California visited Nelson's home in Oakland, California, which was under close FBI surveillance. On this occasion, the scientist turned over to Nelson a complicated formula dealing with the Radiation Laboratory's research into the military use of atomic energy. A few days later, surveillance disclosed that Steve Nelson turned over an envelope (presumably containing the Radiation Laboratory information) to one of his regular contacts, namely Peter Ivanov, Soviet vice counsel in San Francisco. On 10 April 1943, further surveillance coverage of Nelson revealed that an unidentified man visited the Nelson residence and gave Nelson $50,000 in payment "for an assignment well done."

The San Francisco office of the FBI scrambled to identify this man who shortly thereafter proceeded to take a train across country, presumably bound for New York City. The New York office of the FBI was notified. James R. Malley, chief of the Internal Security Squad of the New York office selected two special agents, Warren R. Hearn, Kenneth R. Routon, and me, to assist in this important identification. The three of us proceeded to Newark, New Jersey, to board the train coming from the West Coast. We boarded the train in Newark, made contact with the San Francisco special agents, and took over surveillance of the unidentified man.

The train proceeded into Penn Station, where the unidentified man was met by a chauffeur in a black sedan which proceeded north up Fifth Avenue to a building which we identified as being a Soviet private school for children and residence quarters for Soviet personnel. A review of photographs of Soviet diplomatic personnel identified the unknown subject as Vassili M. Zubilin, third secretary (later second secretary) of the Soviet Embassy in Washington, D.C. We identified Zubilin as being a general in the Soviet NKVD and responsible for directing the Soviet atomic energy espionage efforts in the United States.

Our special agent trio that first identified Zubilin rapidly began to expand as the twenty-four hour surveillance coverage of Zubilin continued. By early 1945, our special counter-espionage squad had grown to as many as sixty-eight special agents, all working in secrecy from the other operations of the NYC FBI office. We selected the name "Comintern Apparatus," as the name of the case, and our reports to the FBI headquarters and the Manhattan Engineer District were dispatched under this name. When Special Agent Warren R. Hearn, who had been assigned primary responsibility for the case, got ill and had to be transferred to the Memphis FBI office to recuperate, I took his place.

After Zubilin, other subjects were identified including Arthur A. Adams, a Soviet engineer who had illegally entered the U.S. through Canada and was operating as an NKVD Soviet espionage agent under a business cover. Adams turned out to be a key subject. Adams' first assignment in the United States was as early as 1919. He was caught in that turbulent period of the Palmer Raids and deported "voluntarily" two years later. His next mission to the U.S. was in 1927 as an official representative of AMO, the Soviet Union's first automobile plant. In 1932 he was back in the U.S. as a member of a group negotiating with Curtis Wright for the purchase of airplanes. Adams' next assignment was in 1936 working both for Red Army Intelligence and the NKVD. This time Adams was assigned to inspect the espionage network posts in New York City, Washington, Pittsburgh, Detroit, and points West in order to improve discipline, tighten procedures, and plant a small seed of fear in order that defection would not enter their minds. Adams had talked of his close relationship with Lenin. Upon his return to Moscow, Adams' work was apparently approved by the Soviet leaders, including Stalin.

Now Adams was ready for his most important assignment. In 1938, Adams was back in Canada awaiting his call to duty in the United States. It came in April 1938. Adams was assigned to replace Colonel Boris Bykov, resident director of several American espionage groups operating on behalf of the Soviets. Bykov was called back to the Soviet Union and reportedly executed after Whittaker Chambers broke with communism and Soviet espionage in April, 1938. Adams had the considerable task of salvaging the demoralized American apparatus, especially after the 1939 Non-Aggression Pact. Adams was able to cross the Canadian border with a false passport and check into the Peter Cooper Hotel in New York City, from which headquarters he operated on behalf of the Soviets until 1945.

At the first opportunity, the FBI agents working on the case were able to review the contents of Adams' brief case. Copies of certain items in the brief case were turned over to the Manhattan Engineer Project in California, and these specialists alerted the FBI that some of the material submitted clearly showed that Adams was getting close to secrets of the atomic bomb. Needless to say, our surveillance of Adams became more and more important. The Justice Department was advised, but we did not have sufficient evidence to proceed against Adams for espionage activities. We were told to keep up the surveillance.

Adams, a professional Soviet espionage agent, soon became aware that he was under round-the-clock surveillance. I received a call at 2:00 A.M. in my apartment, telling me that Adams had disappeared. I told agents that I would join them in the search for Adams. We checked all of Adams' close contacts, the airports, train stations, and bus depots. We recalled that one of the agents who had been on the Adams surveillance had been transferred to the Chicago office. We instructed this agent to immediately proceed to the Chicago train station and check all incoming trains from New York City to determine if Adams was a passenger, since all passengers going to the West Coast had to change stations in Chicago to catch the trains going west. This time we hit the jackpot. Sure enough, Adams had tried to escape by train to the West. The Chicago agent picked up Adams in Chicago and further surveillance of Adams was undertaken by the Chicago office. Adams took the next train west, and it was learned that his destination was Portland, Oregon. Adams departed the Portland train station and proceeded to the docks where a Soviet ship was docked. As Adams approached the gang plank, a number of agents from the Portland FBI office formed a cordon and Adams, fearing arrest, turned around, caught a cab, went to a movie, and then returned to New York City by train where we again instituted twenty-four hour surveillance. Fortunately, we never lost Adams again while I was in charge of the case. Later on, he did escape to the Soviet Union, however.

The agents assigned to this Comintern Apparatus case worked on the average of two to five hours per day overtime (as did other agents throughout the FBI). They were not paid one cent for overtime during the war years or given compensatory time off. When I see and hear vicious, unwarranted attacks on the FBI, I burn because I could relate so many stories of FBI agents' extreme dedication and loyalty to our country. I am sure the close coverage the FBI gave to the Soviet espionage operations severely hampered. discouraged, and prevented them from obtaining the vital secrets prior to our successful testing of the atomic bomb.

The Manhattan Engineer District tested the atomic bomb successfully for the first time in July 1945 at Alamorgordo, New Mexico. On 6 August 1945 we dropped the first atomic bomb on Hiroshima, and on 9 August 1945 the second atomic bomb was dropped on Nagasaki, Japan. Japan surrendered formally on 2 September 1945 aboard the battleship *Missouri* in Tokyo Bay.

The Soviet Union finally obtained the secrets of the atomic bomb (the trigger mechanism or implosion device which was able to set off the bomb) through Julius and Ethel Rosenberg. With this information, they were able to produce and successfully test their first atomic bomb in September 1949, four years after America. American intelligence had previously estimated that the Soviets could not produce their first bomb before 1953. Thereafter, the nuclear buildup began between the East and West.

While FBI agents were working long hours protecting the atomic bomb secrets from Soviet espionage agents from April 1943 to July 1945, top officials of the Roosevelt administration, reportedly including Alger Hiss of the State Department and Harry Hopkins of the White House staff were using their official status to help in shipping key information and scientific materials relating to atomic nuclear technology to the Soviet Union. Here is the story which has been conveniently swept under the rug.

If the Soviets had been able to perfect the atom bomb before we did, I am certain the Soviets would have used it to defeat Hitler and then blackmail or coerce the Free World into Marxist-Leninist Communist subjugation. We would now be living in a "new world order" under Soviet control.

Former Major George Racey Jordan was a liaison officer working closely with the Soviet Purchasing Commission at the Air Deport in Great Falls, Montana, a key departure area for lend-lease material to the Soviet Union from January 1943 to September 1944. When it became more and more difficult to get lend-lease material to the Soviet Union by Murmansk-bound ships convoy because of German submarines, Great Falls became more and more important. It was urgent to get American planes to the Russian front. Planes were flown by USAAF pilots to Great Falls, winterized for operational use in sub-zero weather, and flown to Alaska, where Soviet pilots took over for the long flights to European Russia. Somewhere along the line, a decision was made to carry freight in the bombers, and this is where the trouble began. It was Major Jordan's job to inspect the planes when they were ready to take off for Alaska and give them clearance. At first he kept notes of his observations on backs of odd envelopes and then copied these notes on sheets of paper. By 1944, his concern was such that he began to keep a detailed diary, including the names of all Soviet personnel passing through. Some of Major Jordan's concerns reached intelligence sources, and on 13 March 1944 a special agent of Counter Intelligence Corp (CIC) was sent to Ladd Field to interview Jordan. Jordan advised that the Soviet Union had made a practice of shipping freight to Moscow through the Alaskan Wing. This had been going on for about two years. For the year 1943, the total freight shipped through Great Falls to the Russians was 768,254.2 pounds. (This can be compared to 433,112 pounds from 1 January 1944 to 5 March 1944.) Major Jordan pointed out that there was also an unusual amount of diplomatic mail sent to Russia through great Falls. All of this was protected from censorship by diplomatic immunity. The agent conducting the interview of Jordan recommended that a prolonged interview be conducted with Jordan, that his records be scrutinized for information of a security nature, and that he be contacted regularly. He further recommended that the facts be given due consideration to contacting the State Department, so that corrective measures could be taken.

There is no record that Jordan's recommendation was heeded. Three months later, on 16 June 1944, Charles E. (Chip) Bohlen of the State Department, requested a copy of the CIC report of the interviews with Major Jordan. Twenty-two days later, the State Department forwarded to the second secretary of the Soviet Embassy detailed instructions on the procedure for handling non-diplomatic mail and on non-lend-lease freight. The second secretary promised that henceforth there would be no more violations. This second secretary was none other than Vassili M. Zubilin, Chief NKVD General in charge of Soviet espionage activities in the Western Hemisphere, especially for atomic espionage in the United States. Of course, Zubilin lied, and it was determined that on 20 September 1944 another irregular shipment went through Great Falls.

Apparently, the irregularities at the airport at Great Falls, Montana were swept under the rug for several years and nothing serious was done about them. This was undoubtedly due to the fact that it was well known that Roosevelt had said of Stalin, "If I give him everything and ask nothing in return, *noblesse oblige*, he won't try to annex anything and will work with me for a world of peace and democracy." Harry Hopkins, assistant to Roosevelt at the White House, said of Stalin at a giant Madison Square Garden Rally for Russian War Relief: "We are determined that nothing shall stop us from sharing with you all that we have." This statement was met with cheers from the large audience. No wonder there was pressure on Lend-Lease and from Lend-Lease to release to the Soviets strategic materials necessary for the atomic program.

This can of worms was opened up in the spring of 1949 when ex-Major George Racey Jordan, the liaison officer at Great Falls, heard a radio broadcast about a few grams of uranium which had disappeared from the Argonne Laboratory, an Atomic Energy Commission installation in Chicago. The U.S. Senate was involved in an investigation to determine whether the missing uranium was stolen or lost. Major Jordan remarked to a friend, "If they are looking for uranium, I can tell them about a thousand pounds that got away." This casual remark created considerable activity in the newspaper columns and, thereafter, Major Jordan became a key witness before the House Committee on Un-American Activities (HCUA). The committee chairman, Frank S. Tavenner, insisted that the committee investigate these charges and obtain the full story from Major Jordan. Major Jordan testified:

> The air-freight movement was getting heavier, and in 1943 important Russian people used to go through with five or six suitcases. I didn't stop them at that time because I thought maybe it was legitimate. But, when they started sending the suitcases without people, I got interested; and sending fifty suitcases with armed couriers didn't seem proper and didn't have diplomatic immunity so far as I could see. I let the first two or three batches go through, and inquired of the State Department and the War Department whether the bags had

diplomatic immunity. I couldn't get an answer from the State Department, but I did out of the War Department; and they said I was to be helpful to the Russians in every way.

Major Jordan, in his testimony, identified Alger Hiss of the State Department and Harry Hopkins of the White House as having a hand in expediting the shipments to Russia. The record showed that the following items were shipped by Lend-Lease to the Soviets through the Great Falls shipping base:

9,681 lbs. of beryllium metal;
72,535 lbs. of cadmium alloys;
834,989 lbs. of cadmium metals;
33,600 lbs. of cobalt ore and concentrate;
13,766,472 lbs. of aluminum tubing vital for construction of an atomic pile;
7,384,282 Lbs. of graphite;
25,352 Lbs. of thorium salts and compounds;
228 Lbs. of beryllium salts and compounds;
2,100 Lbs. of cadmium oxide;
18,995 Lbs. of cadmium metals;
29,326 Lbs. of cobalt compounds; and
806,941 Lbs. of cobalt metal and scrap.

HCUA investigator Donald T. Appell took the stand. His testimony was direct and reflected thorough investigation procedures. Appell's testimony revealed that he had come up with far more than a prima-facie case. Major Jordan had been telling the truth, and United States authorities had been incredibly naïve.

Roosevelt's assumption that Stalin would do no wrong had severe repercussions outside the United States. In Istanbul in 1944, a U.S. military attaché was contacted by Major Akhmed, Assistant Soviet Military Attaché, stationed there. He had been recalled to Moscow and feared for his life, recalling the infamous purge trials. Major Akhmed volunteered to the American military attaché that he had important data on Soviet operations in the U.S., including penetrations of the Manhattan Project by various Soviet agents. The U.S. attaché followed what he believed to be the standard procedures of that time, suggesting that the Soviets could do no wrong. The U.S. attaché went so far as to disclose the Major Akhmed contact to the Soviet military attaché. Learning of the disclosure in time, Major Akhmed, the intended defector, turned himself over to the Turkish Security Service, who promptly debriefed him and gave him refuge, thus saving his life. By 1947, American recognition of the Soviet threat was obvious and the Turks made the defector available for debriefing by the U.S. military attaché. His information would have been extremely valuable in 1944. By 1947, it merely confirmed to the U.S. intelligence community what it had missed.

TWENTY-THREE

Harry S. Truman Administration
12 April 1945-January 1953

In January 1945, Harry S. Truman became vice-president of the United States to serve with Roosevelt for his fourth term. Truman served only about three months as vice-president when he was catapulted into the presidency by the death of Roosevelt on 12 April 1945. Truman had very little background or political experience to take on the tremendous responsibility of the office of president. His primary experience had been as U.S. Senator from Missouri from 1934-1945. Because of ill health, Roosevelt did not have the time or the inclination to acquaint his vice-president with the pressing political problems facing the country. Truman had to take over the awesome task as president with the help of the Roosevelt White House and State Department staffs, which were, for the most part, considered liberal, one-world oriented, and apparently were not able to comprehend that our Soviet "ally" could be a threat to the free world.

By 1944, the Soviet army had retaken the Baltic States Estonia, Lithuania, and Latvia from the retreating German army. By 1944, the advancing Soviet armies also had taken over control of Rumania, Bulgaria, and Hungary. In 1945, due to the Teheran and Yalta agreements, the Soviet armies took over East Germany, and Poland. In 1945, the Communist Korean Party of Labor established a Communist dictatorship in North Korea, and the Mongolian People's Republic was forced into the Soviet Union. Truman cannot be held responsible for these losses to communism, but he inherited them from Roosevelt. Beginning with the 1945 Potsdam Conference, Truman had to take responsibility for his own wrong political decisions.

It was no surprise that the July 1945 Potsdam Conference between Stalin, Truman, and Churchill was also a disaster for the West because this conference put the stamp of approval on the Teheran and Yalta decisions which sealed the fate of millions of Eastern Europeans, forcing them to remain under Soviet domination following World War II.

The development of the atomic bomb was the most important top secret of the early 1940s. The first successful explosion of an atomic bomb was at Alamogordo, New Mexico on 16 July 1945. Secretary of State James Byrnes was with Truman at the Potsdam Conference when the successful testing took place. It apparently took several days for the information about the successful testing to reach Truman. On 24 July 1945, President Truman decided to relate this important information about the successful testing to Stalin.

Stalin is reported to have replied that he was glad to know of the successful test and hoped the U.S. would make use of the bomb. Evidently, Stalin already knew these facts. Truman authorized the atomic bomb to be dropped on Hiroshima on 6 August 1945, which helped to bring the war against Japan to an early conclusion and undoubtedly saved many American lives.

In September 1945, Elizabeth Terrill Bentley, a longtime courier for a NKVD-KGB Soviet espionage apparatus, voluntarily provided the New York office of the FBI with voluminous information concerning the operations of two Soviet espionage rings operating in the U.S. during and before World War II. She spent a long time with FBI agents identifying thirty-three members of the Nathan Gregory Silvermaster ring and seven members of the Victor Perlo group. These individuals had furnished classified information on a regular basis to our wartime "ally," the Soviet Union, even though they knew that the Soviet Union was no true friend of the United States. These individuals held key positions in key government agencies such as the Defense Department, the State Department, and the Commerce Department.

Four special agents in the field, William A. Branigan, Dwight M. Smith, James R. Malley, and me, specializing in security matters, were called to FBI headquarters on special assignment in September 1945 to verify the considerable information being furnished by Bentley. After two months of careful checking, we never found one instance where the informant was inaccurate in the information she had furnished.

Bentley was a graduate of Vassar College. She was drawn into the Communist party through her membership in the American League Against War and Fascism. After a period with the open Communist party in the mid-1930s, Bentley had been assigned to underground activities and became the assistant and paramour of Jacob Golos, a member of the inner circle of the CP USA and a KGB (Soviet Intelligence Service) agent. They engaged in espionage operations and had numerous contacts with key government employees in Washington. In 1943, when Golos died, Bentley carried on alone as the espionage courier between Soviet agents and government employees from whom she collected secret government information for the Soviets.

But the hard work of the FBI was wasted when there were no successful prosecutions of the subjects accused by Bentley for the capital offense of espionage. There was not even sufficient corroborating evidence to obtain grand jury indictments. The only prosecutions were of William Remington, a War Production Board employee, and Alger Hiss, a top State Department official, who were both convicted of perjury rather than espionage. The FBI did help to remove these individuals from government employment as quickly as possible, however.

While on special assignment to FBI headquarters in Washington D.C., I was assigned to prepare a detailed summary report for the U.S. attorney general on the activities of Andrei Schevchenko, an engineer for Amtorg, the New York Russian Commercial Trading Co., a cover for a number of Soviet espionage agents. Schevchenko was an agent for GRU (Red Army Intelligence). The FBI had amassed considerable evidence against Schevchenko, who was busy during the war years collecting classified information from American citizens in the Buffalo and Philadelphia areas about aircraft production at the Bell Aircraft Co. and military matters generally. My report clearly showed that we had considerable evidence against him and informants willing to testify, but Truman, through his State Department and Justice Department advisers, feared international repercussions if we tried a Soviet national for espionage. These were trying times for conscientious special agents of the FBI, working uncompensated overtime and not seeing the guilty punished for their crimes.

Prosecution was finally initiated in 1948 against Alger Hiss. Hiss eventually served forty-four months of a five year sentence, but escaped more severe punishment. During the prosecution of Alger Hiss, Truman, instead of reviewing the evidence against Hiss, chose to support Hiss by referring to the Hiss case as being a "red herring." This was a slap in the face of the FBI which had performed an outstanding investigation in a difficult case.

Another key political mistake made during the Truman administration was the switch of support from the longtime pro-American government of General Chiang Kai-shek to Marxist-Leninist guerrilla leaders Mao Tse-tung and Chou En-lai, who were waging civil war from the north. These rebel leaders were described as agrarian reformers who would rule China better than the warlords then in control. The so-called "China Lobby" and other pro-Communist forces were quite persuasive. This switch of support caused mainland China, with one billion inhabitants, to fall under Marxist-Leninist control when General Chiang Kai-chek and his army were finally forced to flee to Taiwan on 8 December 1949. Only the future will tell, but this political blunder may be the most serious one made during the Truman administration.

Will the People's Republic of China become the world leader of Marxist-Leninist struggle for world control in place of the Soviet Union, thus bringing on a new "cold war?" Only time will tell.

Truman arbitrarily removed General Douglas MacArthur from command of the United Nations Forces in Korea on 11 April 1951 because MacArthur wanted to decisively win the Korean War. The war dragged on and finally ended in a stalemate, with North and South Korea divided at the thirty-eighth parallel, the same position held by both sides prior to the North Korean attack on South Korea. Was Truman's decision to remove MacArthur based on the secret National Security Council Memorandum #68, adopted during the Roosevelt administration, which called for a policy of containment rather than victory when fighting against communism? The record shows that the Korean War cost 54,246 lives and resulted in 103,284 wounded with no victory.

Truman finally responded to the considerable publicity following the disclosures of Bentley, Chambers, and others regarding Communists working for the U.S. Government. In November 1946, Truman appointed a temporary commission on loyalty to be guided by the attorney general. The president instructed the commission to study the problem and to report findings and recommendations to him. In a March 1947 report, the commission noted the inordinate presence of allegedly disloyal persons in executive agencies in the past and at that time. It urged vigorous corrective action.

Accordingly, on 21 March 1947, Truman issued Executive Order 9835, which made it mandatory that every employee in and applicant for employment in any department or agency of the U.S. government undergo a loyalty investigation. The standard for employment and removal from employment was that "all evidence [shows] reasonable grounds exists for the belief that the person involved is disloyal to the government of the United States." In 1952, the standard was changed to indicate that "on all the evidence, there is reasonable doubt as to the loyalty of the person involved." Anyone whose loyalty was in doubt was separated.

There was a dispute as to whether the Civil Service Commission or an executive agency with its own investigative facilities, or the FBI, would complete loyalty investigations where a preliminary check at any stage revealed the presence of a compromising factor. Truman's aides noted he favored the Civil Service Commission. They said he wanted to "hold the FBI down" because he feared the FBI was the "Gestapo." Truman relented when he was convinced by others that the FBI had superior facilities and a historical role in investigating espionage and Communist activity. Therefore, any case indicating Communist activity or otherwise revealing compromised loyalty, as described in the order, was sent to the FBI.

Truman made some extremely important foreign policy decisions which were in the best interest of the United States and the Free World. Between 1947 and 1949, the Truman administration was rebuilding American military strength and erecting alliances abroad aimed at countering Communist expansion in Europe. Among these measures were the Marshall Plan to rebuild European economies and the National Security Act of 1947 that established the Air Force, the Central Intelligence Agency (CIA), and combined the military branches in a new Defense Department. The North Atlantic Treaty Organization (NATO), which represented a formidable European buffer against the Soviet Union during the cold war, was founded in April 1949. The Central Intelligence Agency had the responsibility of "coordinating, evaluating, and disseminating intelligence affecting national security." Truman established the National Security Agency (NSA) on 24 October 1952. Truman was instrumental in launching the Marshall Plan in June 1947, which later became known as the Truman Doctrine. These timely initiatives provided assistance to a number of European countries, including Italy, Greece, and Turkey, and probably saved them from Soviet take-over.

Another important step in the containment of Marxist-Leninist communism under the Truman administration was the prosecution of top leaders of the CP USA by Attorney General Tom C. Clark, beginning in 1949. These leaders were brought to trial under the Smith Act of 1940 which made it a crime to advocate the overthrow and destruction of the government by force or violence. Eleven members of the national board of the CP USA were convicted in 1949, and their convictions were later upheld by the U.S. Supreme Court. Prosecution of more than eighty additional Communist leaders throughout the U.S. followed.

These prosecutions opened the eyes of Americans to the menace of Marxist-Leninist communism. Other free-world countries were extremely interested in the way America took action against the Communist menace. These prosecutions forced the CP USA to go underground, and the action greatly disrupted the membership activity and the effectiveness of the party.

TWENTY-FOUR

Dwight D. Eisenhower Administration
January 1953-January 1961

In the fall of 1940, Dwight D. Eisenhower, then a lieutenant colonel, was invited to a small dinner party at the Olympic Hotel in Seattle, Washington. Two other guests at this dinner were John Boettiger and his wife, the former Anna Roosevelt Dall, daughter of President Franklin D. Roosevelt. Reportedly, the next morning, Anna called her father and told him of the genius she had discovered in an army uniform. Within a few days, Eisenhower was ordered to Washington for an interview at the White House. A few weeks later, Eisenhower, back in Ft. Lewis, was made chief of staff of the third Infantry Division. In March 1941 he became Colonel Eisenhower and was made chief of staff of the ninth Army Corps. In June 1941, he was made chief of staff of the United States third Army. At the end of September 1941, Eisenhower became a brigadier general.

Five days after Pearl Harbor, Eisenhower was called to Washington and met with General George C. Marshall on 14 December 1941. Marshall brought Eisenhower into war planning at the highest level. On 16 February 1942, Eisenhower was made assistant chief of staff of War Plans Division. On 9 March 1942, Eisenhower became the first head of the Operations Division of the War Department General Staff with the grade of major general.

On 11 June 1942, Eisenhower was given command of the European Theatre of Operations, and, thereafter, regularly had luncheons and dinners with Winston Churchill at 10 Downing Street.

In July 1942, Eisenhower was elevated to lieutenant general. On 11 February 1943, less than two years from the time he was a lieutenant colonel, Eisenhower became a three star general. Ten months later, although he had never had a combat command and had never commanded a battalion, General Eisenhower was made commander in chief of the Allied forces in Western Europe. People who knew Eisenhower during this period report that it was his personal charm and political genius that proved so successful for him.

Eisenhower came out of World War II in the American public's mind as a great soldier and a man who won the war by his superb military generalship. We have seen how Eisenhower was promoted over the most competent combat commanders in the U.S. Army, such as General George C. Patton. It is reported that Eisenhower had a hatred of all German soldiers, whether part of the elite Nazi SS troops or just ordinary soldiers. If unconditional hatred toward defeated Germany typified the official Allied position, it was Eisenhower who transformed the abstract into the concrete. When millions of Germans surrendered during the closing days of the war, Eisenhower ordered that they be incarcerated in prison camps hastily constructed without shelter or other comforts, without medical supplies or aid, without sanitary facilities of any kind, and without sufficient food and water to maintain minimal health. The camps were nothing more than open fields, surrounded by barbed wire, in which German prisoners stood ankle-deep in muck and human waste. Inmates frequently included not only defeated soldiers but also civilians, the aged, the sick, amputees, women, and children. Dysentery, septicemia, typhus, typhoid, and other diseases swept through the camps. Equally terrible were the prisons under the administration of the French army in which Germans were held for future use as slave laborers in the reconstruction of France.

What is particularly shocking is that not only did Eisenhower order this abomination, but he perpetuated it by frustrating all attempts at alleviating the catastrophe as it developed. While the Allies were awash in an abundance of food, tents, and medicine, Eisenhower complained of a non-existent shortage. General Patton blasted Eisenhower for using "Gestapo methods" against German prisoners and accused him of trying to decimate "the only semi-modern state in Europe so that Russia can swallow the whole." Under Eisenhower's regime, the Geneva Convention on the humane treatment of prisoners was ignored.

Colonel Dr. Ernest F. Fisher, a World War II combat veteran, estimated that,

> starting in April 1945, the United States army and the French army casually annihilated about one million men, most of them in American camps. Eisenhower's hatred produced the horror of death camps unequalled by anything in American military history an enormous war crime.

Based on the protocols of the Teheran, Yalta, and Potsdam Conferences, Eisenhower was responsible for carrying out the criminal operation known as "Keelhaul." In this notorious action, directly ordered by Eisenhower, the commander in chief of the Allied forces in Western Europe, millions of anti-Communist Russians and Ukrainians living in Western Europe, some of whom escaped the USSR at the time of the Bolshevik Revolution, were seized by American and British troops and shipped off in trucks and cattle cars to Soviet-occupied Eastern Europe. Stalin, needless to say, was delighted. Huge numbers of people were butchered on the spot. The rest were sent to die in labor camps throughout the Soviet empire.

Apologists for General Eisenhower later pleaded that he was innocent of this crime in as much as he was only "following orders" from Washington. It has been reported that Eisenhower is *the only man* who was ever allowed to have his picture taken with Stalin (just the two of them together) at the tomb of Lenin.

Eisenhower, during his eight years in office, had ample opportunity to help roll back the advancing Soviet Tide. He failed to take the proper action on a number of occasions when he was in the position to do so, even though he had a hundred to one advantage in nuclear armaments. For example, even though Eisenhower had successfully campaigned on a pledge to work for the liberation of Eastern Europe, he failed to intervene in any manner during the Hungarian revolution in 1956, when the Hungarian people tried bravely to free themselves from Soviet subjugation. President Eisenhower reportedly refused even the simple request for four United States Red Cross planes, bearing U.S. insignia, to land at the four airports the Freedom Fighters had won with their blood to bring medical supplies to their wounded. Had Eisenhower granted this small request for humanitarian aid, it would have been a symbolic gesture to show the world that America stood for freedom.

When North Vietnam fell under Marxist-Leninist control in 1954, there was probably not much that Eisenhower could have done. On the other hand, Eisenhower was persuaded by pro-Communist advisors, especially in the State Department, to switch support from President Batista, in Cuba, to rebel Communist-guerilla leader Fidel Castro, resulting in the defeat of Batista and the takeover of Cuba by Castro on 1 January 1959. Cuba was the first country in the Western hemisphere to become a Marxist-Leninist base for Soviet operations. There is no doubt that the Eisenhower administration was to some extent responsible for this great loss.

In September 1959, Eisenhower held a Camp David summit meeting with Soviet Premier Khrushchev. Face to face diplomacy with the Soviet Union became the preference of each succeeding president. After his Camp

David meeting with Khrushchev, Eisenhower told reporters, "I want to prove that we are not aggressive, that we seek nobody's territories or possessions; we do not seek to violate anybody else's rights. We are simply trying to be a good partner in this business of searching for peace." It is reported that Eisenhower never discussed with Khrushchev the growing body of evidence that Castro was intent on making Cuba the first Soviet proxy in the Western Hemisphere.

Patton was one of the outstanding generals of World War II. During August 1944, Patton's third Army smashed German defenses and rolled across France in a lightning advance. Within sight of the German border and the lightly defended Siegfried line, his forces ran out of gasoline and ammunition. Eisenhower sent supplies earmarked for the third Army to British commander Marshal Bernard Law Montgomery for an airborne invasion of Holland, code name, "Market Garden." The Montgomery plan proved to be a disaster, costing 17,000 British and American lives, while Patton's third Army, in September 1944, was halted, even though willing and able to drive into Nazi Germany and destroy what remained of Hitler's already badly beaten armies. "It was my opinion that this was the momentous error of the war," Patton later wrote.

Forty years after the end of World War II, and the death of Patton, it is possible to conclude that the judgments and decisions Patton made were, in some instances, more intelligent than those of Eisenhower. Stopping Patton's army from a thrust into Germany prolonged the war and cost more Allied casualties. It also gave the Soviets the necessary time to advance toward Germany from the east and to occupy Eastern Europe. Eisenhower's later decision to allow the Soviets to capture Berlin had been defended on the grounds of saving lives, but he threw away lives earlier by halting Patton in August 1944. Keeping Patton from taking Prague proved equally favorable to the Soviets.

Eisenhower, early in his presidency, was forced by public opinion to restore some degree of semblance of national security to the country, and in 1953, he issued Executive Order 10450 which supplanted Executive Order 9853. The earlier order was promulgated by Truman on 21 March 1949, mandating that every government employee and applicant undergo a loyalty investigation. The new E.O. 10450 promulgated by President Eisenhower did not limit the investigation to loyalty but set a new standard requiring that "the employment of the person is clearly consistent with the interests of national security." This ended the possible stigma of being terminated because of compromised loyalty.

TWENTY-FIVE

The Pros and Cons of the Counterintelligence Program Cointelpro

1956-1961

On 8 March 1956, Director J. Edgar Hoover of the FBI briefed Eisenhower, Vice-president Nixon, Attorney General Brownell, and other high-level U.S. government officials at the White House. Hoover told them that the FBI sought to infiltrate, penetrate, disorganize, and disrupt the CP USA using numerous techniques to obtain information and evidence. In July 1956, William Cornelius Sullivan, then chief of the Central Research Section of the Domestic Intelligence Division, proposed that special counter-intelligence operations be directed against the CP USA and that the operation be considered by a committee, "to discuss and formulate and recommend a systematic program for the disruption of the CP USA." Sullivan specifically recommended that I be approved to handle the program because of my work as supervisor-in-charge of the Overthrow and Destruction of the Government Unit and the Smith Act Unit from 1946 to 1956.

After my approval to handle this special program against the CP USA, I recommended that the program be closely supervised and that only one special agent in each of the twelve largest membership districts of the CP USA be responsible for the program in that office. In other words, only twelve special agents in the field and I at FBI Headquarters would be handling the program.

I stressed from the beginning that the techniques to be employed should be for disruption and not harassment. Each proposed technique had to be approved by FBI headquarters before implementation.

During the five years I was the supervisor-in-charge of COINTELPRO, the Soviet Union was involved in extreme anti-Semitism. The charge primarily against Jews in the Soviet Union was carried out under the name "Cosmopolitanism." One of the techniques we used under the COINTELPRO was to anonymously send copies of well-documented newspaper and magazine articles describing the extent of anti-Semitism in the Soviet Union to Jewish members of the CP USA. This, over a period of time, was extremely successful, since a large percentage of the membership of the CP USA in Brooklyn, the Bronx, Chicago, and Los Angeles was Jewish. When it became clear to the Jewish members of the CP USA that the Soviet Union was no paradise, especially for Jews, they began to drop out of the party. We also used informants in the party who were especially coached to bring up questions at meetings which often caused meetings to break up in discord and pit members against each other. We had informants in the highest levels of CP USA who could point out weaknesses in the party operations.

When I went to FBI headquarters as a supervisor in 1946, the membership of the CP USA was 74,000. After the Smith Act trials of the CP USA leadership and five years of COINTELPRO, the membership in 1961 had dropped to less than 5,600.

While I supervised COINTELPRO from 1956 to 1961 against the CP USA only, William C. Sullivan, who originated the program, had absolutely no input into its operation. As section chief of the Central Research Section, Sullivan began to have dreams of becoming director of the FBI. In many ways he tried to impress Hoover with his superior intellect and his antipathy toward communism. As Sullivan delivered more speeches on communism on behalf of the FBI, he came into contact with liberal people in the educational field who felt that communism was no longer a menace and that the FBI should not be giving communism the priority it was receiving. Before too long, Sullivan began soft-pedaling the menace of communism and was substituting the Ku Klux Klan and white hate groups as more dangerous than the CP USA. This change Sullivan carefully kept hidden from Hoover.

On an inspection trip abroad in the 1960s, Sullivan actually confided to an FBI legal attaché in Europe that someday he would become director of the FBI. By 1961, Sullivan had so captivated the attention of Hoover with his writings and lectures that Hoover promoted Sullivan to assistant director of the Domestic Intelligence Division. For some reason, Sullivan began to view me as a possible threat to his dreams of becoming FBI Director. Sullivan was now the head of the division of which my COINTELPRO Unit was a part, and thus, I was subject to Sullivan's commands. Shortly after Sullivan's promotion I was reassigned from COINTELPRO, without any notice or discussion, to handle new FBI action under the Communist Control Act. Another supervisor was placed in charge of the COINTELPRO Unit.

When I was in charge of COINTELPRO from 1956 to 1961, Hoover approved all my techniques and operations against the CP USA. After I moved to other assignments, the COINTELPRO was expanded by Sullivan to involve other organizations than the CP USA, including the Ku Klux Klan, white hate groups, black hate groups, the Socialist Workers Party (the leading Trotskyite Communist party), and Communist front organizations and individuals, including Doctor Martin Luther King, Jr.

Throughout 1961 and most of 1962, Sullivan and I had little contact. In November 1962, I prepared a memorandum for Hoover which recommended that the FBI give consideration to discussing with top government officials, such as the attorney general, secretary of state, and others, the idea of establishing a special condensed school of approximately one week to teach government officials in contact with Soviet and other Communist officials throughout the world a course on communism which would prepare them for such contacts. The course would be taught by experts on communism in the FBI and other intelligence branches of the armed forces. My memo had to be routed through assistant director Sullivan. After reading my detailed memo, Sullivan called me into his office and said he was not going to forward it to the director. I insisted it must be sent through and that if he objected, he could add an addendum, as long as he desired, pointing out his objections. Sullivan dismissed me with the statement to forget all about the memo. Obviously, Sullivan did not want to be pitted against me in the eyes of the director on the subject of the menace of communism.

Again in early December 1962, I sent through another memo to Hoover. This memo, in essence, recommended that a secret video (to be used at some later date) be prepared with Hoover interviewing our two top informants in the CP USA, namely Morris and Jack Childs, brothers who had been informants at the highest levels of confidentiality in the CP USA. I knew Hoover would be in favor of such a video. Again, Sullivan denied my request, and I insisted that it go through with his addendum explaining why he did not agree with the idea. Again, he told me to forget the memo. I knew that Sullivan's decision to block the memo was against all former FBI policy, but I felt that I had no chance of competing in a battle with Sullivan, with whom Hoover had become so favorably impressed.

Because of these two memos, I began to feel that Sullivan would react towards me in some sudden manner very soon. It came over the Christmas holidays in December 1962. Sullivan apparently wrote a memo recommending that I be promoted to the Inspection Staff of the FBI. My past work had been exemplary and I deserved such recognition, he wrote. Sullivan knew that

Assistant to the Director Alan H. Belmont (the number three man in the FBI) was a good friend of mine, and he knew that Belmont would not approve such a memo because Belmont knew that I desired to stay in Washington and had turned down chances to go on the Inspection Staff a number of times. But Sullivan waited until Belmont was on Christmas leave and expedited his memo. The director approved the transfer. I decided not to contest the transfer as Sullivan would find other techniques to use against me. Apparently, he wanted me out of Washington and no longer a threat to him. This new position on the Inspection Staff required inspections of FBI field offices all over the country—six weeks away from home and one week at home. No one had ever been placed on the Inspection Staff at almost fifty years old, as I was. Due primarily to difference of opinion between Sullivan and me, I retired from the FBI on 12 August 1963, shortly after my fiftieth birthday. An FBI agent was then able to retire at age fifty, with twenty years of service; I had twenty-three years of service.

Even though Sullivan was carrying on expanded COINTELPRO operations, some with Hoover's approval, some without, Hoover, in June 1970, appointed Sullivan to replace Cartha D. DeLoach as assistant to the director for all investigative activities, the number three executive job in the FBI. Sullivan was getting closer to his goal of FBI director.

Hoover did not recognize Sullivan's faults or ambitions until just before September 1971, when he locked Sullivan out of his office, removed him from his number three spot in the FBI, and forced him to retire. Hoover, in a letter to Louis B. Nichols, his former number three executive, confessed:

> As for Sullivan, your comments concerning him were certainly true, I only wish that I had been able to spot his instability long before I did. When the crisis finally came, I moved swiftly and forced him into retirement. I personally think that I have

been blessed with an exceptionally outstanding staff of executives through my administration of the Bureau with the exception of Sullivan. You certainly were tops when you were in the Bureau and I have never questioned your loyalty since you left it.

COINTELPRO received some unfair criticism. For example, it was accused of being a secret program of the FBI using a code name to identify it. But the top officials of the U.S. government were advised of the program prior to and during its establishment. The so-called "code name" was a shortening of the exact title to save money in our teletypes to the field. This was done in all other cases handled by the Bureau.

COINTELPRO was discontinued in 1971, the year Sullivan was forced into retirement by Hoover. During its operation from 1956 to 1971, 2,370 COINTELPRO proposals were implemented (56% were directed against the CP USA). During testimony before the Senate Church Committee, the FBI director, then Mr. Kelly, on 10 December 1975, pointed out that these fifteen years were an era when the FBI was handling an average of 700,000 investigative matters per year. If the 2,370 proposals are divided by the total investigative matters, the quotient is .000226, meaning they represented less than twenty three thousandths of one percent of the Bureau's investigative efforts during that period. This vanishingly small segment of its operations that been over-emphasized by FBI detractors to claim that the bureau operated in complete disregard of Constitutional liberties.

TWENTY-SIX

John F. Kennedy Administration
January 1961-22 November 1963

One of the first disasters of the Kennedy administration was his decision involving Cuba which, in effect, nullified the Monroe Doctrine. Here is the story which should now be told in full to the American people.

On 2 December 1823, President James Monroe proclaimed the Monroe Doctrine in order to protect the nations of the Western Hemisphere from conquest by European empires. The Monroe Doctrine was upheld for 135 years by the government of the United States, and the Western Hemisphere appeared to be safe from the type of encroachments by the Soviet Union that had subjugated many Eastern European countries during the 1940s. However, in 1958, the United States, under Eisenhower, unfortunately decided to withdraw its support of President Fulgencia Batista of Cuba, a long-time friend of the United States, and began to increase its support to Fidel Castro. Castro was a long-time Communist outlaw with his rebel revolutionary forces fighting in the Cuban mountains. This support finally allowed Castro to take over Havana, Cuba, on 1 January 1959. Castro lost no time in concentrating his power throughout Cuba through atrocious repressive measures and with the help of the Soviet Union. In early 1961, the United States government, under President Kennedy, who had just taken office, belatedly began to recognize that Cuba was becoming a loyal surrogate of the Soviet Union and broke off relations. Castro retaliated immediately by openly disclosing his alliance with the Soviet Union and the

Soviet Bloc. It soon became apparent that the Monroe Doctrine had been violated by a back door revolutionary operation, because, as of 1961, the Soviet Union, a European empire, had its foot firmly planted in Cuba, a Western Hemisphere country.

In April 1961, an anti-Castro invasion force, which had been trained and financed for some time by the U.S. CIA, landed in the Bay of Pigs, Cuba. Unbelievably, President Kennedy, who had taken office just three months before, refused to provide the invasion forces with the promised air support because of Soviet and Latin American pressures and liberal advisors warning him of adverse world opinion. The Bay of Pigs carefully planned invasion effort collapsed in part reportedly because President Kennedy did not fulfill the promise of support made before he took office. The result was a humiliating loss of prestige throughout the entire world.

In 1962, the Soviet Union brazenly began to build missile sites in Cuba and provided Castro's army with troops, planes, and submarines. Alarmed, President Kennedy, on 22 October 1962, served notice that the U.S. was willing to risk a major war with the Soviet Union. The U.S. established a blockade which confronted Soviet vessels and demanded that the Soviet Union remove its missiles, weapons, and troops from Cuba. The threat to U.S. security was real. Much credit and praise were given to President Kennedy at the time for bravely standing face to face with Khrushchev and causing Khrushchev to blink and back down. Now we understand that Kennedy reportedly secretly promised, as part of the package agreement with the Soviet Union, that the United States would never again attack or invade Cuba. This was "peace" at any price. No wonder Khrushchev jumped to sign the agreement. Now you know why Castro is still in power in Cuba and still helping to subvert other countries in the Western Hemisphere. Incidentally, the agreement did not provide for verification and it is not known, even at this date, whether all of the Soviet missiles were removed from Cuban soil. Castro's Cuba has been an expensive vassal state; expensive for both the Soviet dictatorship and particularly for its downtrodden Cuban population. After the Soviet fragmentation in 1991, Cuban support dwindled and finally came to an end.

Immediately after his failure to overthrow the Communist regime of Fidel Castro, President Kennedy agreed to meet Soviet Premier Khrushchev in Vienna in June 1961. Khrushchev believed he could turn Kennedy's inexperience to his advantage, and that the Bay of Pigs failure had placed the American president in a position of weakness. "Khrushchev behaved toward Kennedy," Peter Mooney notes, "with a directness that had been lacking in his dealing with other statesmen." Whereas, before, the relationship between Kennedy and the USSR had been fairly relaxed, it was now strained.

In rapid succession following the Vienna summit, the Soviets moved to deny the West access to West Berlin and started construction of the Berlin Wall. These were moves which the Kennedy administration refused to challenge.

President Kennedy, along with the leaders of West Germany, France, and England, share responsibility for lack of appropriate surveillance and proper communication and action when they passively allowed the East German Communists on the night of Sunday, 13 August 1961 (part of a long Assumption Day weekend) to finish building the infamous Berlin Wall, which sealed off the last exit from Communist Europe to the Free World. Had the three (West Germany, France, and England) of the Four Power Allied Authorities been fulfilling their responsibility to the Free World, they would have sent tanks and could have stopped the building of the Berlin Wall, which obviously was in violation of the Four Power Berlin Accords. The building of the wall effectively stopped the exodus of up to 50,000 Europeans each week fleeing to the West from Communist Europe.

By 1960, the political climate in the country began to change after the death of Senator Joseph McCarthy, whose Senate hearings against Communists backfired badly because of his ineptitude and poor leadership. The Kennedy administration, during its short period, opened the door so pro-Soviets and persons soft on communism could obtain positions in the U.S. State Department.

Shortly after John F. Kennedy was elected president in 1960, he brought his brother, Robert Kennedy, into his administration as attorney general. The liberal establishment now believed it was possible to bring back former security risks into government service. Dean Rusk, President Kennedy's choice for secretary of state, and Bobby Kennedy, his choice for attorney general, even before taking office in January 1961, met with the deputy director of the Office of Security of the State Department to discuss the possibility of obtaining security clearance for Walt Rostow. The deputy director explained why Rostow, who had been denied appointment twice during the Eisenhower administration, could not be appointed until certain procedures were followed. The position being sought by Rostow was to head the Policy Planning Staff, a position requiring Senate confirmation following an updated FBI investigation. This position was subject to special standards set up by the U.S. Intelligence Board. The head of the Policy Planning Staff was to formulate cold war psychological strategy concerning the Soviet Union.

It appeared that the main reason for the meeting with the deputy director was to evaluate him and not primarily to get Rostow into the State Department. After the meeting, it became clear to Rusk and Bobby Kennedy that the deputy director would have to go if they had any hope of getting their security tainted friends into the State Department. Thus began a long, courageous, eight year struggle by the deputy director to defend his position in the State Department.

The first step in eliminating the deputy director as an obstacle was to order him into a special project of reviewing old security files. While so assigned, the first of Secretary of State Rusk's appointees began to obtain employment in the State Department without proper security investigations.

Next, the State Department Office of Security was "reorganized," and the deputy director's position was eliminated. The deputy director was given a reduced position not related to the security field after refusing to resign. During the fourteen months the deputy director was detailed to the special project, the State Department granted waivers (deferring background checks) on 152 new officials in the department. During the eight years of the Eisenhower administration, the secretary of state used only five such waivers. Many security clearances were allowed to bypass the Division of Evaluation. By this method, the White House was able to slip Walt Rostow into the State Department. While in the department, Rostow laid out goals for American foreign policy along the lines of unilateral disarmament, world government, and accommodation with the Communist world. The same lack of thorough security clearance investigations continued in the State Department throughout the Kennedy administration and the Johnson administration.

President Kennedy, while riding in a procession in Dallas on 22 November 1963, was shot to death by an assassin firing from an upper floor of a building. The alleged assassin, Lee Harvey Oswald, was killed two days later in the Dallas city jail by Jack Ruby, owner of a striptease dance hall. At forty-six years of age, President Kennedy became the fourth president to be assassinated, and the eighth to die in office. The death of President Kennedy catapulted his Vice-President Lyndon Baines Johnson into the presidency.

TWENTY-SEVEN

Lyndon Baines Johnson Administration

November 1963-January 1969

Johnson was elected to the Senate in 1948. At the height of his power as a Senate leader, Johnson sought the Democratic nomination for president in 1960. When he lost in the race to John F. Kennedy, he surprised even some of his closest associates by accepting Kennedy's offer to run with him on the ticket as vice-president. With a plurality of only 118,574 votes, Kennedy carried the election of 1960 over Vice-President Richard M. Nixon. Vice-President Johnson was riding in another car in the motorcade when Kennedy was assassinated. Johnson took the oath of office of president in the presidential jet on the Dallas airfield.

President Johnson inherited Robert S. McNamara, the secretary of defense under President Kennedy. Keeping McNamara in this position during his entire administration was one of the worst mistakes of Johnson's years in the presidency. McNamara recently admitted in his memoirs that the Vietnam War was a terrible mistake, and he, as secretary of defense, enforced most of the policies that led to the defeat. This allowed the Soviet Union to take over the strategic Cam Ranh Bay base in Vietnam, the largest naval forward deployment base outside the Warsaw Pact, and gave the Soviets control over key areas of the western Pacific Ocean.

The Vietnam conflict finally came to an end in a most embarrassing and humiliating retreat of the United

States on 30 April 1975. This was during the Gerald R. Ford administration. The Vietnam conflict years were indeed rough times, especially for the Johnson administration. So-called "experts" have commented on what went wrong. Most of them are still sweeping under the rug certain facts that should be squarely faced so we will never again get involved in such a "no win" conflict.

The conflict in Vietnam was never officially declared a war, and remained merely a "police action." Because of this, the pro-Communists and anti-American elements felt relatively safe in militantly demonstrating against our involvement and were able to openly fraternize with the enemy. If this police action had been declared a war, these elements would have been guilty of treason whenever their actions gave aid and comfort to the enemy. In the future, Congress must exercise its prerogative and declare war against the enemy, particularly if the enemy is a Communist enemy like North Vietnam.

The responsibility for the deaths of more than 58,000 Americans, the thousands more who were wounded, and the many thousands whose lives were shattered and altered in the jungles and rice paddies of Vietnam should weigh heavily on those civilians who laid down the controversial "rules of engagement" that were imposed on our fighting men in Vietnam during the Johnson and Nixon administrations. Military men who have commented on these rules of engagement have said that no other force in modern history was ever called upon to fight under such severe restrictions, which actually aided the enemy. U.S. superiority in both air and artillery fire power were deliberately not exploited in North or South Vietnam.

The rules of engagement were first promulgated by Secretary of Defense Robert S. McNamara under President Johnson and were revised off and on through May 1971. These rules were kept secret for years and not revealed until Senator Barry Goldwater placed them in

Congressional Record on 6 June 1975. These rules of engagement were so misguided that commanding officers who led their forces into action were impelled to break faith with their men by not providing them the protection they needed and deserved. Here are a few of the rules of engagement which compelled our American heroes to fight with one hand tied behind their back:

1. Assaults on hamlets, villages and urban areas in both Vietnams known to shelter enemy forces generally had to be preceded by loud speaker warnings and leaflet drops. This rule, of course, encouraged the Communist forces to occupy populated areas knowing they would be appropriately warned of attack in advance.

2. Infantry units could open fire only when the enemy was positively identified and in close contact. Sniper and mortar fire were not counted as "contact" unless, "such fire interferes with the scheme of maneuver, is inflicting casualties or damage to equipment." This rule handed the initiative to the enemy and often forced American troops to accept damage before retaliating.

3. Air attacks on dams, locks, dikes, and targets within 1.5 miles of Hanoi, Haiphong, and the buffer zone along the Chinese border were banned without prior approval of the Joint Chiefs of Staff. Because of this asinine rule, most of the anti-aircraft missile sites around Hanoi and Haiphong were placed on dikes.

4. Aerial assault on North Vietnam airfields was forbidden if a plane with a third nation's markings was present, something the North Vietnamese quickly figured out, and governed themselves accordingly.

5. Air and artillery strikes against targets in certain areas had to be withheld until specifically approved by the province chief, district chief, sector commander, or a battalion or higher command. Obvious targets for air and artillery strikes were more often than not sighted by aerial observers. As soon as the communist troops realized they had been spotted, they dispersed, and by the time permission was granted, the enemy was long gone.

The question logically follows: why hasn't Robert S. McNamara, especially since his recent memoirs, and the other top ranking civilians responsible for the rules of engagement been brought before a congressional committee and made to explain the reasons for the outrageous conduct of the Vietnam conflict?

Four years elapsed between the Kennedy assassination on 22 November 1963 and the June 1967 Glassboro, New Jersey, summit between President Johnson and Soviet Premier Alexei Kosygin. During that period, the Soviet and Chinese Communists supplied massive amounts of military hardware to the North Vietnamese. That equipment led to the wounding and killing of thousands of American servicemen in a "war" in which an American military victory was subordinated to international and domestic political considerations.

President Johnson, in his memoirs, disclosed that he decided to meet Kosygin in the small New Jersey college town in order to prevent protesters, for or against the Vietnam War, from besieging the gathering. At the summit, President Johnson sought to convince the Soviet premier of his sincerity in wanting to begin immediate talks about limiting nuclear weapons and about negotiating a settlement of the Vietnam War. Kosygin wished to talk about the Middle East and the Israeli destruction of the Soviet trained and supplied Egyptian army in the Six Day War that occurred three weeks before the summit. President Johnson recalled that, "each time I mentioned missiles, Kosygin talked about the Arabs and Israelis."

At the start of the summit, Kosygin contended that Hanoi was willing to begin talks for a negotiated peace if the U.S. called a halt to the bombing of North Vietnam. President Johnson agreed to stop the bombing, but he noted that no response ever came from Moscow or Hanoi. President Johnson maintained, "Despite many subsequent exchanges with the Soviets on Vietnam, they never gave us an answer, nor did anything ever come from Hanoi."

Like Eisenhower in the 1956 Hungarian uprising, Johnson, in August 1968, took no steps to gain support for intervention or try to muster Free World support for the brave people of Czechoslovakia who rose up to overthrow their Soviet oppressors. Brezhnev, in suppressing the Czech uprising, invoked a new doctrine called the "Brezhnev Doctrine," which called on all Communist countries to come to the aid of a Communist country if it was threatened from without or within by anti-Communist elements. This new doctrine forced the Warsaw Pact satellite countries for the first time to send armed units to assist the Soviets in putting down the Czech revolution. This made it impossible for the captive Eastern European nations to independently regain their freedom from Soviet control until the fragmentation of the Soviet Union that began in 1989.

With all the problems confronting his administration, Johnson chose not to seek re-election in 1968.

TWENTY-EIGHT

Richard M. Nixon Administration
January 1969-9 August 1974

Republican Richard M. Nixon, with his conservative and anti-Communist views, came into the presidency with the high hopes of a majority of the American people. He won the 1968 presidential election over Democrat Hubert H. Humphrey and Independent George C. Wallace. Nixon had been a member of the U.S. House of Representatives from 1946 to 1950, a U.S. senator from 1950 to 1952, and vice-president under Eisenhower from 1952 to 1960. He ran for president against John F. Kennedy in 1960 and lost by only 118,574 votes. There were reportedly strong grounds for belief that Democratic machines in Chicago and Texas "manufactured" the necessary votes for Kennedy. Nixon declined to disrupt the post-election calendar. Nixon earned his anti-Communism mantel while a member of the House Committee on Un-American Activities when it investigated Alger Hiss, the top State Department official who was charged with espionage activities on behalf of the Soviet Union. This investigation led to the later conviction of Hiss.

Under President Nixon, even with his alleged conservative and anti-Communist views, the Soviet Union made considerable advancement.

President Nixon, relying on the advice of Henry A. Kissinger, his national security adviser and secretary of state, implemented the doctrines of "Déntente" and "Mutually Assured Destruction" (MAD). These doctrines were established because Kissinger and other "one-worlders" and foreign policy global strategists believed that if the Soviet Union was allowed to reach parity with the United States in conventional and nuclear armaments, then it should no longer feel insecure, encircled, or threatened by the West. In addition, the Nixon administration encouraged our multi-national corporations and our international banks to open up communication and trade with the Soviet Union and render assistance wherever possible.

Dr. Anthony Sutton, in his book entitled *The Best Enemy Money Can Buy,* identified more than 160 companies involved in "free trade" with the Soviet Union during the twenty-five year period from 1960 to 1985. While the doctrines of "détente" and "mutually assured destruction" were being implemented, the Soviet Union not only reached parity with the United States in nuclear and conventional armaments, but surpassed the United States in a number of categories.

Perhaps the largest single project built by the western capitalists in the Soviet Union was the KAMAZ-Kama River integrated heavy duty truck plant. This plant, the largest in the world, is spread over thirty-six square miles situated on the Kama River. It has a capacity of more than 100,000 multi-axle ten ton trucks, trailers, and off-the-road vehicles. This transfer took place under President Nixon and his national security adviser, Henry Kissinger, and was approved even though the plant obviously had military capability. The products from this plant played a key role in the Soviet invasion of Afghanistan in 1978.

President Nixon was committed to wind down the U.S. role in the Vietnam War. Nixon trained and equipped South Vietnamese to do their own fighting. The number of American ground combat forces in Vietnam fell steadily from 540,000 when Nixon took office, to 0 in 1973, when the military draft was ended. U.S. air power was continued.

Nixon improved relations with Moscow and reopened the long closed door to mainland China with a good-will trip there in February 1972. In May 1972, Nixon visited Moscow and signed agreements on arms limitations and trade expansion and approved plans for a joint U.S.-Soviet space mission in 1975.

In the November 1972 elections, President Nixon swamped the Democratic ticket headed by Senator George McGovern of South Dakota with a plurality of 17,999,528 out of 77,718,884 votes cast.

Trials and tribulations for the Nixon administration began to develop with the botched burglary of the Democratic National Headquarters in the Watergate apartment complex in Washington, D.C. in June 1972. In January 1973, hints of a Nixon cover-up emerged at the trial of six men found guilty of the Watergate burglary. With a Senate investigation under way, Nixon announced on 30 April 1973 the resignation of his top aides, H.R. Haldeman and John D. Ehrlichman and the dismissal of White House counsel John Dean, III. Dean retaliated by being the star witness at televised Senate hearings, exposing both a White House cover-up of Watergate and massive illegalities in Republican fund-raising in 1972. The hearings also disclosed that Nixon had routinely tape recorded his office meetings and telephone conversations.

On 10 October 1973, Spiro T. Agnew resigned as vice-president, then pleaded no contest to a negotiated federal charge of evading income taxes on alleged bribes. Two days later, Nixon nominated the House minority leader, Representative Gerald R. Ford of Michigan, as the new vice-president. Congress confirmed Ford on 6 December 1973.

In the summer of 1974, President Nixon met in Moscow with Soviet leader Brezhnev and reached preliminary nuclear arms limitation agreements. Nixon admitted that his summit meetings with Brezhnev in

Moscow in 1974 were in part an outgrowth of the Soviet Union's rapidly developing superiority in strategic nuclear weapons. In his memoirs Nixon wrote,

> I knew the Soviets were moving much faster than we were in this area. Unless we got some agreement soon, we might face a situation in which we would be weaker than the Soviets in the eyes of our allies, our friends and neutral countries. Therefore, in addition to pinning Brezhnev down to a new agreement by the end of 1974, I specified that we should be talking about reductions and not just limitation of nuclear weapons."

Within a month after this summit meeting, Watergate ended the Nixon presidency. On 24 July 1974, the Supreme Court ordered Nixon to surrender subpoenaed tapes. On 30 July, the Judiciary Committee referred three impeachment articles to the full membership. On 5 August 1974, Nixon bowed to the Supreme Court and released tapes showing that he halted an FBI probe of the Watergate burglary six days after it occurred. It was, in effect, an admission of obstruction of justice, and his impeachment appeared inevitable. Nixon resigned on 9 August 1974, the first U.S. president ever to do so. A month later, President Ford issued an unconditional pardon for any offenses Nixon might have committed as president, thus forestalling possible prosecution.

The 1973 and 1974 continuing attacks on the Nixon administration gave impetus and opportunity to the pro-Communists, pro-Soviet, and "one worlder" ideologues to intensify their assault on the internal security forces of the United States which had been set up to protect the security and sovereignty of our country.

In April 1973, long before Nixon was forced from office, the Internal Security Division of the Department of Justice was abolished. In June 1973, the Subversive Activities Control Board was dismantled. In 1974, the U.S. attorney general's list of subversive organizations was eliminated. A new retirement law was passed in the early 1970s, forcing all FBI agents who were fifty-five years old, with twenty years of service, into mandatory retirement; thus many special agents with irreplaceable counter-intelligence and anti-Communist expertise were lost to the service of their country. During May and June 1973, under pressure, the CIA dismissed hundreds of senior officers with anti-Communist and counter-intelligence expertise. Since 1973, under continuing pressures, many irreplaceable CIA foreign service officers were forced into early retirement. Shortage of experienced officers is one of the reasons for the publicized failure of the CIA in such areas as Iran, Ethiopia, Afghanistan, Libya, Lebanon, and Angola.

Vice-president Gerald R. Ford became president of the United States when President Nixon resigned and left Washington for his home in California. Nixon's five and a half years in office were complex. They presented successes and failures in his dealings with the Soviet Union and international communism.

TWENTY-NINE

Gerald R. Ford Administration
9 August 1974-January 1977

Under President Ford, the attack on our U.S. intelligence agencies continued unabated. On 14 January 1975, the House Internal Security Committee was abolished. In 1977, the Senate Internal Security Sub-Committee of the Judiciary was eliminated as a separate group. In 1975, the Intelligence Community was especially distraught over the drawn out hearing by the Senate Select Committee, headed by Senator Church, and the House Special Committee, headed by Representative Pike. The principal targets of these highly publicized hearings were the FBI and CIA. These hearings dealt further injury to our overall intelligence gathering capabilities by painting the operations of these agencies with a distorted and sullied image.

In March 1976, Attorney General Gerald Edward Levi, who was appointed by President Ford, imposed new domestic security "guidelines," making it virtually impossible for the FBI to carry out an effective internal security operation. The Levi "guidelines," still in effect today with some modifications, prohibit the FBI from probing any group unless it has evidence the organization has violated a federal statute or is planning a violation that threatens great harm and is likely to take place in the near future. On 22 September 1976, FBI Director Clarence Kelley revealed that because of these guidelines the FBI had been forced to reduce its security cases from 21,414 in July 1973 to 626 cases in 1976. In 1979, FBI Director William Webster was reported as saying that as a result of these guidelines literally hundreds of security investigations of the past had been closed. As of 1979, Director Webster admitted that the FBI was then investigating only between twelve and sixteen domestic organizations and from forty to sixty individuals engaged in terrorist activity. Because of these guidelines the FBI, since 1976, has almost been prohibited from carrying out its long time responsibility for the internal security of the country and now operates primarily as a federal police organization moving only against violators of federal criminal statutes. The FBI can no longer compile investigative evidence on the potential dangerousness of an individual to the internal security of our country unless he is an immediate threat or is actually engaged in violation of federal law.

In case of a national emergency or war, the FBI cannot operate as it did the first seventy-two hours following Pearl Harbor, when it arrested 3,846 previously-investigated and deemed-dangerous enemy aliens (of Japanese, German, and Italian nationality). These aliens were arrested under previously planned presidential warrants. Because of this prompt wartime action, there was not one case of successful enemy directed sabotage against our country during World War II.

While the debacle against our intelligence agencies at home was taking place under the presidency of Ford, seven countries fell under Marxist-Leninist domination. They were South Vietnam, Cambodia, Laos, Madagascar, Sao Tome, Angola, and Mozambique.

Another mistake of Ford was to retain Henry Kissinger, whom he had inherited from President Nixon, as secretary of state. Despite the Vietnam disaster and the important role the Soviets played in that U.S. defeat, Kissinger continued to prevail on President Ford to pursue "détente" with the Soviets. When Nobel Prize winning Soviet author Alexander Solzhenitsyn, in a 30 June 1975 speech, characterized "détente" as a continuation of the Munich appeasement policies of British Prime

Minister Neville Chamberlain in the 1930s, President Ford acted on the recommendation of secretary of state Kissinger and refused to invite the Russian novelist to the White House.

Efforts by President Ford to conclude a SALT II Agreement with the Soviets did not restrain them from moving into Angola with Cuban proxies.

In a speech given in Detroit on 24 November 1975, Kissinger openly protested Soviet and Cuban involvement in Angola. It should be noted, however, that former Chief of Naval Operations Admiral Zumwalt, in his book, recalled that the secretary of state had admitted to him privately that, "in the light of history, he (Kissinger) will be recognized as the one who negotiated terms favorable to the Soviets."

From 1976 until President Ford's defeat by Jimmy Carter, Henry Kissinger continued to push for approval of the Salt II Agreement. This agreement was officially signed by President Carter and Soviet leader Brezhnev at the June 1979 summit in Vienna.

During the 1976 election campaign, San Francisco played host to a nationally televised debate between President Ford and challenger Jimmy Carter. The most memorable point in the otherwise forgettable confrontation occurred when Ford defended his signing of the Helsinki Accords sanctioning Soviet rule over the captive nations of Eastern Europe. He (Ford) said, "There is no Soviet domination of Eastern Europe and there never will be under a Ford administration." The statement was totally absurd and everyone but Ford knew it. The panelist, Max Frankel of the *New York Times,* charitably gave the president a chance to correct his gaffe. But Ford dug himself an even deeper hole with, "I don't believe that Yugoslavians consider themselves dominated by the Soviet Union. I don't believe the Poles consider themselves dominated by the Soviet Union. Each of these countries is independent, autonomous; it has its own territorial integrity." The Soviet troops in Poland surely knew better. The people of Poland knew better. Jimmy Carter knew better. So did any well-informed American. But the president of the United States showed his abysmal ignorance of world affairs, and it may well have cost Ford the election. It is reported that President Johnson once said of Ford, who was a football lineman at the University of Michigan, that he had done one too many practices without a helmet. He may have been right.

The World Affairs Council of Philadelphia met on 4 July 1976. At this meeting, a new document called "A Declaration of Inter-dependence," was drawn up to supersede our revered Declaration of Independence, signed by John Hancock and other great American patriots on 4 July 1776. This new document proposed the total surrender of national sovereignty, our total disarmament, and even our constitutional rights to bear arms. This 1976 "Declaration of Inter-dependence" was reportedly signed by 104 of our U.S. senators and representatives. In endorsing the "Declaration of Inter-dependence," our 1976 congressmen promised: "We, the undersigned members of Congress support the principles embodied in the Declaration of Inter-dependence of the World Affairs Council of Philadelphia, and urge their study and discussion to promote American policy and initiative which respond to new global conditions of interdependence."

What a difference 200 years make.

THIRTY

Jimmy (James Earl) Carter Administration

January 1977-January 1981

When Jimmy Carter took office in 1977, only one in three people in the world lived in freedom. There were forty-three "free" nations, forty-eight "partly free" nations, and sixty-four nations which were "not free." Of the sixty-four nations not free, most of them were under Marxist-Leninist domination or some form of Marxist Communist dictatorship.

Particularly troubling is the sad story of Nicaragua, because the Carter administration was quite active in helping in the overthrow of General Somoza by supporting the Communist Sandinistas who took over and established Marxist-Leninist control. Under President Somoza, Nicaragua formerly had been anti-Communist and friendly to the United States. Thus, Nicaragua became Communist with the help of President Carter, just as Cuba became Communist with the help of President Eisenhower. Two Western Hemisphere countries fell to Marxist-Leninist communism with the help of the U.S. government. Sandinista guerillas, leftists who took their name from General Sandino (a Nicaraguan guerrilla in the 1920s), who led forces opposing U.S. Marines trying to establish order in that country, launched an offensive in Nicaragua in May 1979. After seven weeks of fighting, Samoza fled the country on 17 July 1979. The Sandinistas assumed power on 19 July 1979. In September 1979, President Carter had the temerity to welcome to the

White House Sandinista Communists Daniel Ortega, Alfonso Robelo, and Sergio Ramirez. The meeting, according to White House officials, "Centered on ways to strengthen the basis for a cooperative relationship between the United States and Nicaragua based on mutual respect."

Two days after the 1979 Carter-Sandinista meeting, the *New York Times* published a letter from Earl E.T. Smith, the U.S. ambassador to Cuba from 1957 to 1959. Smith said that, "Nicaragua is Cuba all over again," and that the same American government agencies and media that brought Fidel Castro to power in 1959 had also brought the Sandinistas to power in 1979. To those saying that substantial U.S. financial aid must be sent to the Sandinistas to keep them from embracing communism, Smith replied,

> The present regime in Nicaragua is already Marxist oriented. Internal security and police powers are under Thomas Borge, who is a Marxist and the leader of the most radical of the Sandinista factions. Borge has gone so far as to pledge support publicly to revolutionary movements in neighboring El Salvador, Guatemala, Honduras, and Costa Rica.

On 21 February 1977, *U.S. News & World Report*, carried an article just one month after the Carter administration took over control of the government. According to the article,

> A profound change in the way U.S. foreign policy is made has emerged in the wake of Henry Kissinger's departure from the State Department.

The article further stated,

> The President, despite his inexperience in world affairs, has made it clear that he intends to exercise ultimate responsibility for formulating the basic lines of American foreign policy. There will be no "Carter's Kissinger."

The president relied not on one man, but on a team to help him shape and implement his international program. The article further stated that President Carter had gone to considerable lengths to insure that the National Security Council staff in the White House, under Brzezinski, did not become the powerhouse that it was under Kissinger in the Nixon years. Going even further, Carter reorganized the National Security Council, replacing seven committees with two. Kissinger's power stemmed mainly from his chairmanship of all of the key committees.

Members of the Trilateral Commission took charge of foreign policy-making in the Carter administration. Active or former members of the Trilateral Commission headed every key agency involved in mapping U.S. strategy for dealing with the rest of the world. The list includes President Carter at the White House, Cyrus Vance at the State Department, Harold Brown at the Defense Department, and W. Michael Blumnenthal at the Treasury Department. Altogether, sixteen high posts in the administration were held by men and women associated with the organization. There was much speculation about the Trilateral Commission. Some saw this concentration of power as a conspiracy at work. The U.S. Labor Party alleged the commission was engineered by multi-national companies in order to dominate American foreign policy.

What is the Trilateral Commission? Who is behind it, and what does it do?

> The Commission was formed four years ago (in 1973) by David Rockefeller chairman of Chase Manhattan Bank, with the help of Zbigniew Brzezinski, a Columbia University specialist on international relations. Its name stems from the fact that its members represent countries in the three-sided Western Alliance: The United States, Western Europe, and Japan. Rockefeller's motivation was his concern over a growing crisis within the Western Alliance. He and his collaborators felt that

then Secretary of State, Henry Kissinger, was pursuing a dangerous policy by stressing U.S. relations with its adversaries, Russia and China, to the neglect of relations with Japan and America's allies in Western Europe. Rockefeller's aim was to reinforce Alliance unity through the Commission and its roughly 200 members. These handpicked individuals came from business, academic and media groups.

Brzezinski took a leave from Columbia University to serve as director of the organization. He became the driving force behind the Commission—'both the wind and helmsman' in the words of one observer. Since its founding, the Commission has met about once a year to discuss international issues. The founders, anxious to have a liberal Southerner in their ranks, invited Jimmy Carter, then the Governor of Georgia to join.

For Carter, it marked the beginning of his education in international affairs, providing him with what he called 'a splendid learning opportunity'— partly under Brzezinski's tutelage. Carter's election to the Presidency and his appointment of fifteen fellow members to key Administration jobs put the Trilateral Commission on the map.

The subcommittee on criminal laws and procedures of the Senate Judiciary Committee prepared a report in late 1978 which pointed out how far the attacks on our security agencies had gone since they began with Nixon and continued in Ford and Carter. The report was captioned, "The Erosion of Law Enforcement Intelligence and Its Impact on the Public Security." This report said, in no uncertain terms, that U.S. law enforcement and investigative groups no longer had the authority to investigate and/or gather information on persons or groups who posed an imminent danger to the security of the United States and its citizens. Police departments all over the country reportedly destroyed their so-called intelligence files and disbanded their special departments engaged in developing information on dangerous individuals and organizations who might be involved in terrorist or anarchist type activities. Apparently these officials were convinced that they did not have the authority to investigate until the bomb exploded, the public official was assassinated, or the anti-government rally became an actual riot resulting in bloodshed.

FBI morale began to plummet following the prosecution of John Kearney, former New York office supervisor of Squad forty-nine, by the Carter administration. Kearney retired from the FBI in 1972, after twenty-five years of service with an immaculate record and the respect and affection of his colleagues. In 1977, five years after his retirement, Kearney was called before a federal grand jury on charges brought by officials of the Civil Rights Division of the Department of Justice, which had long been hostile to the FBI. Kearney was indicted on five separate counts for his activities involved in an intensive manhunt to apprehend federal fugitives connected with the Weather Underground organization, the most vicious group of terrorists yet to operate in America. They were responsible for many bombings, including the U.S. Capitol, the Pentagon, and a number of police headquarters, which resulted in the death of at least one police officer and injuries to many others.

Kearney's use of special investigative techniques were similar to those which had been regularly performed by hundreds of other FBI agents for over forty years, under the approval of five different presidents. One year after Kearney's indictment and his expenditure of $157,000 in legal fees and related costs, the Department of Justice dismissed the indictment because it finally recognized it had no case. The department refused to reimburse Kearney for any of his staggering defense costs. It was John Kearney whose civil rights were violated rather than the friends and relatives of the Weather Underground fugitives.

To add further insult to injury to the security agencies of our country, the Carter administration began what turned out to be a three year persecution of two former top officials of the FBI. On 10 April 1978, W. Mark Felt, former associate director, and Edward S. Miller, former assistant director of the Intelligence Division of the Federal Bureau of Investigation, were indicted under a sixty year old statute as revised in Section 241 of the Civil Rights Act of 1969. Felt had loyally served the FBI from 1942 to 1973, and Miller from 1950 to 1974.

The one count indictment charged them with being engaged, during 1972 and 1973, in a "conspiracy to violate the civil rights of friends and relatives of Weatherman Underground fugitives by utilizing techniques of surreptitious entry." The specific charge was that five different residences were entered, four of which were occupied by "above ground" supporters and/or sympathizers of the terrorist group. The fifth home was occupied by parents of one of the Weatherman fugitives.

Felt and Miller, as top officials of the FBI, were carrying out their sworn duties for the protection of our country when they authorized the field special agents in the New York City area to make efforts to locate and apprehend dangerous Weatherman Underground fugitives. Surreptitious entry techniques had been carried out for more than thirty years under the approval of five presidents and their attorney generals.

Following the indictment, Felt and Miller were subjected to long periods of trial delays, running up their legal defense costs into a staggering amount. Their plea for change of venue was summarily dismissed by a judge whose bias was painfully obvious throughout the pretrial and actual trial proceedings. After seven different sets of trial dates were passed, the trial finally got under way on 15 November 1980, two years, five months and five days after the indictment.

An honest review of this completely biased trial which ended with a one-hour, forty-minute charge to the jury by Judge William B. Bryant, will show that Felt and Miller had no chance for acquittal from the very beginning. The charge itself all but called for a guilty verdict. Finally, on 6 November 1980, the jury of eight women and four men, sequestered for the duration of the two month actual trial, reached its verdict after eight hours of deliberation. The verdict was "guilty as charged." Felt and Miller faced up to ten years imprisonment and $10,000 fines. Fortunately for Felt and Miller, Ronald Reagan was elected president in the November 1980 elections. When Judge Bryant sentenced Felt and Miller on 15 December 1980, he obviously recognized the changing political situation. Felt was fined $5,000, and Miller $3,500, with no prison sentence. Mark Felt said, "I don't regard this as a relatively light sentence. I am a convicted felon and I regard it as a very serious blemish on my career."

On 15 April 1981, following his recovery from the assassination attempt, President Ronald Reagan publicly announced that he had signed an Executive Grant of Clemency on 26 March 1981, wherein he had granted both Felt and Miller a full and unconditional pardon. Unfortunately, the pardon did not wipe out the legal effect of the conviction, so Felt and Miller were forced to appeal their case. Finally, on 28 November 1983, Judge William Bryant was ordered by the higher court to sign an order dismissing the indictment under which Felt and Miller had been convicted in his court three years before, thus completely clearing the record. Now Felt and Miller could practice law or carry out any other lawful activity since they were no longer tainted by the earlier indictment and conviction. It is strange that more Americans could not have seen this case in its true light and protested this extreme mockery of justice.

The prosecution of these dedicated former FBI officials has a side line that you will find hard to believe. The *New York Times* carried an article on 7 September 1979, reporting that President Carter, citing "humane considerations," commuted the sentences of a Puerto Rican nationalist who attempted to assassinate President Truman in 1950, and of three others who sprayed gunfire from a gallery overlooking the House of Representatives, wounding five congressmen in 1954. In commuting the sentences to time served, the White House said the president concurred with Secretary Cyrus R. Vance that the release of these prisoners would be "a significant humanitarian gesture and would be viewed as such by the international community." Apparently the president and his advisors were not able to distinguish those who wore white hats from those who wore black. All of the prisoners in questions were guilty of terrorist activities, having killed a presidential guard and gunned down five congressmen on the floor of the House. Not one of them was repentant. A United Press International release on 11 September 1979 showed two of the terrorists "lecturing" at the United Nations that day. The caption read:

> Determined and unrepentant Puerto Rican nationalists Lolita Lebron, fifty-nine, and Oscar Collazo, sixty-four, lecture newsmen on revolutionary ethics at a news conference at U.N. Headquarters. Released from prison on December 10th after their sentences for terrorist activities were commuted by President Carter, both vowed to spend the rest of their lives "fighting" for a free and independent Puerto Rico.

On 15 December 1978, the Washington, D.C. press revealed that President Carter announced that he would establish full diplomatic relations with the Chinese Communist regime in Peiping on January first, and break diplomatic ties with the Free Chinese government on Taiwan. Carter welcomed Red Chinese Deputy Prime Minister Teng Hsaio-ping to the White House on 29 January 1979, "to begin working together to enhance the cause of world peace." The Free Chinese government at Taipei on 15 December 1978, declared that

President Carter's recognition of Red China "constitutes a great setback to human freedom and democratic institutions."

The Carter administration was never able to get a Red Chinese commitment not to take Taiwan by force, but went ahead with diplomatic recognition anyway. The Chinese Reds maintained that "the way of bringing Taiwan back to the embrace of the motherland and reunify the country is entirely (Red) China's internal affair."

While Carter was president, eight countries fell under Marxist-Leninist domination, including Angola, Mozambique, Ethiopia, Afghanistan, South Yemen, Nicaragua, Guyana, and Guinea-Bissau. On 1 October 1979, the United States returned "Marxist" Panama sovereignty over the strategic 535 square mile Panama Canal Zone that had been governed by the U.S. since 1904. All U.S. control over the Panama Canal is scheduled to end at noon on 31 December 1999. The absurdity of this giveaway by Carter will become increasingly apparent in years to come.

THIRTY-ONE

Ronald Reagan Administration
January 1981-January 1989

Ronald Reagan always wanted to be a professional actor, and in 1937 he jumped at the offer of a movie contract. In his acting career, he appeared in fifty movies and many television shows. He was an active member of the Screen Actors Guild and headed the labor union from 1947 to 1952 and 1959 to 1960. In his union activities, Reagan learned much about communism and its devious tactics.

After winning acclaim for his speeches in support of Barry Goldwater in the 1964 presidential elections, Reagan turned to a new career: politics. Reagan won election as governor of California in 1966 and re-election in 1970. During his administration (1967-1975), California State taxes were reformed, ending deficit spending and rebating $4.7 billion to property tax payers. He slowed the growth of state government and contained social welfare spending. In the 1980 presidential elections, Ronald Reagan soundly defeated Jimmy Carter by a vote of 43,898,770 to 35,480,948 and an electoral vote of 489 to 49.

Totalitarian Marxism-Leninism aggression had considerable success and very little opposition following World War II, from 1945 to 1980. During this thirty-five year period, an average of one country each year was subjugated and forced to submit to non-democratic Marxist-Leninist control. By 1980, it was estimated that 42% of the world population was living under varying degrees of Marxist-Leninist totalitarian control.

On Christmas 1979, still under the Carter administration, the Soviet Union invaded Afghanistan, and soon became mired down in a prolonged brutal and inhuman effort to bring that country under total Communist subjugation. It appeared that the Soviet tide of successful takeovers might be ebbing. In fact, there had not been one new Soviet or Marxist-Leninist takeover of a Free World country since 1980. In 1983, President Ronald Reagan, in a surprise military move, rescued 1,000 American students on the island of Grenada who were endangered because of Communist unrest and instability. For the first time, a Marxist-Leninist country was returned to democracy, and the Brezhnev Doctrine was not called into action.

During the Reagan administration, sympathy and support were given to freedom fighters and guerilla forces in eight Marxist-Leninist countries who were fighting bravely against overwhelming odds in an effort to reestablish democracy and freedom. These countries were Afghanistan, Angola, Cambodia, Ethiopia, Laos, Mozambique, Nicaragua, and Vietnam.

Reagan received nothing but trouble for his efforts to salvage Nicaragua from Marxist-Leninist control. Right after taking over as president, Reagan, recognizing the growing danger to Central America, suspended economic aid to Nicaragua because of evidence the Junta was aiding left-wing guerillas in El Salvador. Reagan was right. When conservative Nicaraguan businessmen complained in October 1981 that the Junta was turning the nation into a Communist state, the Junta threw the opposition leaders into prison and shut down the opposition newspapers. In April 1985, the U.S. Congress rejected a plea by Reagan for fourteen million dollars in humanitarian aid for the freedom fighters (Contras). The vote had hardly been counted before President Ortega of Nicaragua took off for Moscow to visit his Marxist-Leninist advisers and obtain more aid from them. Trying to help the Contras in Nicaragua to regain their freedom from Marxist-Leninist control was a real headache for President Reagan, and it almost scuttled the Bush administration. The Democratic Congress was dead set against any help for the freedom fighters of Nicaragua.

Reagan understood that the only thing the Soviet leaders recognized was military strength and the initiative to use that strength. He recognized that the United States must be strong enough to withstand a massive Soviet attack. That is why Reagan insisted on the build-up of our military forces, although it was costly. This build-up and the Reagan threat to launch Sky Wars caused the Soviets to back down, and eventually this helped bring about the fragmentation of the Soviet empire. Near the end of the Reagan presidency, the NATO and Warsaw Pact military ratios were still very much out of kilter. The strength of the United States made the difference.

The status of the conventional forces in Europe showed a definite imbalance between the NATO and the Warsaw Pact:

Order of battle	**NATO**	**Warsaw Pact**
Uniformed manpower	5.1 million	6.3 million
Reserves	6.3 million	8.2 million
Main battle tanks	22,000	52,200
Artillery	11,100	37,000
Armed helicopters	780	1,630
Combat aircraft	3,889	7,963

One of the principal endeavors of the Reagan administration from the very beginning was to substantially build up the defense apparatus of the U.S., which had been allowed to deteriorate under the Nixon, Ford, and Carter administrations. However, because of these costly military expenditures and failure to balance the budget during his first six years in office, the federal debt reached the staggering total of over two trillion dollars. Reagan's federal debt for his first six years was reportedly greater than all previous presidents' added together. Yet it can be seen that the Soviet and Warsaw Pact forces were still greater than the Free World forces in Europe.

Gorbachev took over the leadership of the Soviet Union in 1985, the same year President Reagan began his second term. *Time* magazine, in its 9 September 1985 issue, gave Soviet dictator Mikhail Gorbachev the front page cover. In addition to the cover photo, this issue dedicated eighteen pages to an interview of Gorbachev, gave comments on the interview, and provided the Soviets with an opportunity to launch a propaganda campaign to prepare Gorbachev for his first summit meeting with Reagan in Geneva. It is difficult to see how anyone could view this expansive coverage of Gorbachev as being in the best interests of the United States, especially since the questions asked of Gorbachev during the two hour, twelve minute interview were mild, palliative, and self-serving for him and the Soviet Union.

The Soviet propagandists and the Soviet press constantly attacked the United States and the West as imperialists, condemned democratic principles, and were forever making irrational and impossible demands. *Time* magazine should have recognized that Gorbachev was a mature Soviet official and should have been ushered into the real world by being treated in the interview in the same manner as Western leaders were treated by the Soviet press.

Reagan began his presidency in January 1981 by taking a strong anti-Soviet stance. At his first presidential press conference on 29 January 1981, Reagan set a chilly tone. The Soviets, he said, "Reserve unto themselves the right to commit any crime, to lie, to cheat," in pursuit of world domination. No other U.S. president had pursued such a tough foreign policy stance. Then, just three months later, President Reagan adopted a pragmatic course that belied his hostile words; he lifted the ineffective grain embargo that Carter had imposed on Soviet trade after the 1979 invasion of Afghanistan. From the very beginning of the Reagan administration, "Its policy toward the Soviet Union has had a typically Reaganesque twist; harsh ideological rhetoric tempered by moves rooted in an emerging realism. The inconsistency has caused relations between the two superpowers to blow hot and cold. Mostly, they have blown cold."

On 29 December 1981, Reagan imposed pipeline sanctions in response to martial law imposed in Poland. Eleven months later, Reagan lifted the pipeline sanctions. On 8 March 1983, Reagan spoke at the annual convention of the National Association of Evangelicals in Orlando, Florida. Friends and foes of the president called this speech the "Evil Empire" speech in which he said, "There is sin and evil in the world," referring to the Soviet Union as the evil side. On 23 March 1983, Reagan proposed his Star Wars defense system. On 1 September 1983, the Soviets shot down KAL flight 007. Then the Soviets walked out of the arms talks. On 7 May 1984, the Soviets pulled out of the Olympic Games. After this 1984 Soviet boycott, Reagan repeated his willingness to "meet and talk anytime" with Soviet leaders.

It took Reagan's overwhelming re-election triumph in November 1984 to persuade the Soviets that their adversary must be dealt with. The Kremlin began to indicate a new willingness to talk. In January 1985, Secretary of State George Shultz and Gromyko of the Soviet Union met in Geneva and agreed that arms control bargaining should resume. In March 1985, Gorbachev succeeded to power in the Soviet Union, and both sides warmed up to the idea of a summit. On 2 July 1985, the summit meeting was set for November 1985 in Geneva.

President Reagan gave a forty-five minute speech on 8 May 1985 at Strasbourg, France, on the fortieth anniversary of the end of World War II. He spoke before an elected parliament made up of 434 members from the ten nation European democratic community. You would think that the "great communicator" would have had the full support of such an audience. Among other charges, Reagan accused the Soviets of trying to, "Spread their dominance by force." He strongly warned the West not to be complacent about the "Kremlin's military intentions." As Reagan criticized the Soviet Union, about thirty deputies, most from the British Labor Party, walked out of the assembly. About a third of the deputies either joined the walkout, sat silent with arms folded, or waved brightly colored signs that said, "Hands off Nicaragua," "Star Wars No," and "Nuclear Freeze Now."

The 14 December 1987 *US News & World Report* characterized the

> meeting with Gorbachev in Geneva in November 1985, produced the best communiqué ever. It expressed the full American agenda in terms that Americans could understand. For once, we had an agreed document that did not read like translation from Russian. It called, you will remember, for "early progress" toward agreement in precisely the areas that you wished to emphasize; deep reductions in strategic offensive armaments, the elimination of medium-range missiles, the working out of verification arrangements "in parallel" with the negotiation of substantive agreements, the resolution of human rights issues and the establishment of exchange programs emphasizing large numbers of students and young people rather than government officials and KGB technicians. Soviet demands that you abandon SDI were, in Geneva communiqué, regulated to the back burner.
>
> The Geneva communiqué was made possible by the firmness and clarity with which you put forward the American position. It was the product of two days of negotiation culminating in an all-night session and a photo finish. There was barely time to ready the final draft for signature at the concluding ceremony. I remember how pleased you were as we headed back to Washington. Gorbachev, of course, was unhappy at the outcome. His long and sometimes bitter concluding press conference made that clear. And, he simply ignored the un-

dertakings he had signed, as he would later ignore his commitments to a Washington summit in 1986. I'm afraid we let you down in not pressing the full implementation of the Geneva agreement. The momentum you imparted at Geneva quickly dissipated.

Richard Perle, the contributing editor of the above article was described as a former assistant secretary of defense for international security policy, and a resident scholar at the American Enterprise Institute. The article continued with the following information concerning President Reagan's second summit meeting with Gorbachev in Reykjavik, Iceland in 1986:

> The second summit held at Iceland in 1986, was without precedent in the annals of superpower diplomacy. The substantive maneuvering that took place there startled a world accustomed to set-peace summits that were more like mortgage closings—dreary and predictable—than true diplomatic exchanges. At the summits in 1972, 1973, 1974 and 1979, there had been champagne but no bubbles; at Reykjavik, there were bubbles but no champagne.
>
> The Gorbachev strategy at Reykjavik was clever (he is as you've seen, a tough, shrewd negotiator). He went to Reykjavik dangling "concessions" upon strategic and medium-range offensive forces. Then, as you reached out to grasp them, he pulled them back (you could almost see him take his cards from the table), demanding that you abandon SDI (Strategic Defense Initiative) as the price for eliminating medium-range missiles and halving strategic arsenals. In reality, the elimination of medium-range missiles and deep reductions in strategic forces on both sides are hardly Soviet concessions to us; Properly constructed such an outcome would leave us equal. But, Gorbachev has consistently sought to portray the reduction of these weapons as a concession for which we should be prepared to pay.

Gorbachev assumed that after Reykjavik you would collapse under pressure from members of Congress and some of our allies since he had made offensive-weapons reductions contingent on your giving up SDI. I am sure he left Iceland convinced that the SDI program would fall like ripe fruit when he told you that there would be no agreement on medium-range missiles, no strategic arms reduction if you did not throttle SDI with testing restrictions that would preclude its success. His was an offer you could and, with courage and determination, did refuse. And, Gorbachev's strategy, based as it was on a disastrous miscalculation, failed. In the end, when Americans rallied around the SDI program and our allies supported you, he was forced to abandon that strategy. There is a lesson here too; if you make concessions first, in the expectation that your adversary will reward you later with concessions of his own, you may be disappointed. Don't expect him to make that mistake again.

In March 1986, Michael Gorbachev addressed the twenty-seventy Communist Party Congress in the mammoth Palace of Congress within the Kremlin's walls. This was a ten day gathering of Communist and Socialist parties from the Soviet Union and 113 other nations. Gorbachev,

> still in his first year in power confidently pressed his agenda of "radical" economic reform in a five and a half hour speech to 4,993 delegates and a national television audience. The article continued "Gorbachev, fifty-four, lambasted the U.S. in the best Soviet tradition as the "locomotive of militarism." He concluded some unusually candid criticism of predecessors, condemning "the inertness and stiffness" of administration and the "escalation of bureaucracy" of the Leonid Brezhnev era for having done "no small damage" to the homeland.

George Will, the well known columnist, wrote an article for *The Washington Post* dated 12 March 1986, concerning this twenty-seventh Soviet Communist Party Congress. This article, "Gorbachev Will Hasten Soviet Decline," was sagacious:

> The acrid aroma hanging over the Communist Party Congress was the old incense of the Communist church: burnt reputation. Gorbachev trashed the reputation of Brezhnev, as Brezhnev had done to Khrushchev, who did unto Stalin, world without end, amen.
>
> It has been said that the problems confronting the industrialized democracies are solvable by policy changes, whereas Soviet problems require systemic changes. Nothing announced or even foreshadowed at the Congress suggests such change. So the Soviet crisis of congealment will continue, and the Soviet Union will become decreasingly suited to the modern world.
>
> Pat Moynihan says the delicate U.S. task is "managing the decline" of the Soviet Union. For as they come to sense they are doomed, they must become ever more dangerous. Henry Rowan of the Hoover Institution, writing about "living with a sick bear," says the interest of the West is in "letting the Soviet system decay."
>
> The sensible way to respond to Soviet decline is by hastening it. Policy should be; no "détente," and more of the Reagan Doctrine of increasing the cost of the Soviet empire by supporting insurrections at the margin of the empire (Afghanistan, Nicaragua, Angola).
>
> The Soviet Union is no longer (in Churchill's words) a riddle wrapped in a mystery inside an enigma. It is conspicuously an invalid trapped in a bureaucracy drunk on a 19th century fallacy, Marxism. It is a system being driven toward suffocation and anemia, its deserved destinations.

While actual fragmentation of the Soviet Union did not occur until 1991, when Yeltsin replaced Gorbachev as head of the Soviet Union during the Bush administration, most observers say that much credit should be given to the Reagan administration for employing the Reagan Doctrine against the Soviet Union. It took a president like Reagan to confront Soviet Communist tactics. More than 200 years ago, Will Havard, the English actor and dramatist, wrote that "the greatest glory of a free born people is to transmit that freedom to their children." Reagan should be recognized for his efforts in preventing the Soviet Marxist-Leninist leaders from achieving world domination and allowing Americans to have the legacy of freedom.

THIRTY-TWO

George H. Bush Administration
January 1989-January 1993

George Bush served as vice-president during the Reagan years (1981 to 1989). In November 1988, Bush defeated presidential contender Michael S. Dukakis by a vote of 48,886,097 to 41,890,074. On 20 January 1989, Bush was sworn in as the forty-first president of the United States.

Bush, who had been a war hero, had attended the NATO fortieth anniversary meeting in Brussels and the Paris economic conference, had toured Eastern Europe, and had met with Gorbachev, all before taking office. He had shown himself to be an able soldier and skilled diplomat. In his first year in office, Bush faced the Lebanese hostage crisis and an escalating domestic crisis centering around the drug trade.

His second year in office was also a challenge, with unprecedented budget deficits and the crisis among the nation's savings and loans. Defense issues, unemployment, and environmental concerns were also problems for the new president.

In 1991, Bush led the fight to free Kuwait and signed the Strategic Arms Reduction Treaty (START) in July, ending a long-standing arms escalation with the U.S. and USSR. With the Soviet Union crumbling, Bush's success seemed to enhance his status.

Before becoming president, Bush had been a member of two organizations which supported world government. Bush served as a director of the elitist Council on

Foreign Relations (CFR) and as a member of the Trilateral Commission. Senator Barry Goldwater claimed that

> What the Trilaterals truly intend is the creation of a worldwide economic power superior to the political governments of the nation-states involved They propose an international economy managed and controlled by international monetary groups. As managers and creators of the system they will rule the future.

Bush selected members of the CFR to serve in his administration as defense secretary, treasury secretary, attorney general, CIA director, and U.S. ambassador to the United Nations. During the course of his administration, Bush, often referred to the New World Order, but I do not recall anyone asking him precisely what he envisioned the New World Order to be. On 24 May 1989, President Bush, in his fourth foreign policy speech in five weeks, suggested that the decades-old policy of "containment" of the Soviet Union should be replaced by a policy that would welcome the Soviet Union into the world community. In his speech to the graduates of the U.S. Coast Guard Academy in New London, Connecticut, Bush reiterated his "open skies initiative," a proposal first made by Eisenhower in 1955, allowing unarmed surveillance flights over U.S. and Soviet territory.

After weeks of peaceful pro-democracy demonstrations in Beijing, China, tens of thousands of Communist troops, reportedly from inner Mongolia, seized control of Tiananmen Square on 4 June 1989 by killing and wounding hundreds, even thousands, of demonstrators. Many demonstrators were shot, while others were run down by armored vehicles on the Avenue of Eternal Peace, Beijing's main east-west thoroughfare. In Washington, President Bush deplored China's "decision to use force against peaceful demonstrators," and urged "non-violence, restraint, and dialogue." President Bush suspended military sales to the Communist China regime, but only temporarily. Although the Bush administration suspended licenses for four pending arms exports to China, he allowed work on these projects to continue, thereby indicating that the exports would eventually be approved. On 7 July 1989, the State Department lifted a waiver on the sale of four 757-200 Boeing jetliners to China.

Secretary of State James A. Baker III met with Chinese Foreign Minister Qian Qichen on 31 July 1989, in Paris, breaking President Bush's promise that there would be a suspension of high-level contacts. Former President Nixon met Bush in the White House on 5 November 1989 to brief him on his recent trip to China. Nixon, of course, had gone to China as a "private citizen."

Bush bowed to Chinese pressure on 30 November 1989, with a pocket veto of legislation to allow Chinese students stay in the U.S. The House passed this bill 403 to 0; the Senate passed it by a voice vote. The Chinese government strongly protested this congressional action and threatened to suspend the student exchange program if Bush did not veto the bill. This he did by his failure to act on the legislation.

National Security Advisor Brent Scowcroft announced on 9 December 1989, from Beijing, that he and Deputy Secretary of State Lawrence Eagleburger had gone to China as presidential emissaries, "to bring new impetus and vigor" to U.S.-China relations. This visit had not been previously announced. On 18 December 1989, the White House also disclosed that Scowcroft and Eagleburger had traveled secretly to Beijing in July, only one month after the Tiananmen Square massacre.

On 19 December 1989, President Bush lifted his so-called sanctions against the export of three communications satellites to China. A White House statement said that his decision was in compliance with Bush's policy "not to disrupt normal commercial relations with China." It became quite obvious that President Bush's rhetoric against China was at odds with his actions.

On 30 April 1989, Bush reportedly told reporters: "We want *perestroika* to succeed." On 22 November 1989, in his Thanksgiving address to the nation, President Bush expressed the same sentiment more strongly, declaring that, "there is no greater advocate of *perestroika* than the president of the United States."

The architect of *perestroika*, Gorbachev, in October 1989, explained *perestroika* to a group of economists and Communist party officials in Moscow as follows: "The concept, the main idea, lies in the fact that we want to give a new lease on life to socialism through *perestroika* and to reveal the potential of the socialist system." In December 1989, Gorbachev described *perestroika* as "The salvation of socialism, giving it a second breath, revealing everything good which is in this system." By endorsing *perestroika*, Bush was actually embracing totalitarian socialism, not freedom.

Throughout 1989, Bush and his administration advanced the cause of *perestroika* and the Soviet Union in many ways. In March 1989, the Commerce Department relaxed control on the export of certain computers and computer-driven medical devices to the Soviet Bloc. During the same month, with the approval of the Bush administration, six U.S. companies signed a trade agreement with the Soviet Union: Mercator Corp., RJR Nabisco Inc., Eastman Kodak Co., Chevron Corp., Archer-Daniels-Midland Co., and Johnson & Johnson. The agreement provided the legal framework for joint ventures between each of the companies and the Soviet Union. Vladimir Kamentsev, the Soviet Union's top trade official, predicted that the agreement, "Will be a precedent," and will set the stage for at least twenty-five U.S. Soviet joint ventures involving U.S. corporate investments of between $5 billion and $10 billion.

On 20 May 1989, President Bush approved taxpayer-financed subsidies on the sale of 1.5 million metric tons of wheat to the Soviet Union. On 18 July 1989, the Commerce Department lifted export restrictions on a wide range of desk top personal computers, paving the way for their sales to the Soviet Union and Eastern Europe. This decision was assailed by defense Secretary Richard Cheny who said, "I disagree with raising the level of sophistication of those computers sold to the Soviet Union or East Block countries because I do believe it would give them significant capabilities that they do not now possess." Yet on 16 October 1989, Secretary of State Baker told the Foreign Policy Association that the United States is, "Prepared to provide technical assistance in certain areas of Soviet economic reform."

At the Malta summit on 2-3 December 1989, Bush offered Gorbachev U.S. support for observer status in the General Agreement on Tariffs and Trade (GATT), presumably as a prelude to full membership, and other forms of assistance. He expressed support for awarding Russia most favored nation status, provided the Soviets liberalized their emigration policies. On 4 December 1989, Secretary of State Baker told NBC News, "Whatever we do, we are doing because it is in our best interests to see *perestroika* succeed because if it succeeds, we will see a more stable, open and secure Soviet Union."

Nineteen hundred ninety-one was a turbulent year for the Soviet Union with its bitter elections, attempted *coup d'etat* in August, the ousting of Gorbachev, and the emergence of Yeltsin as leader of the fragmented Soviet Union. On 25 December 1991, the Soviet Union broke up after Gorbachev resigned; the constituent republics formed the Commonwealth of Independent States, which the U.S. and other nations promptly moved to recognize.

In the November 1992 election, William Clinton defeated Bush by a vote of 44,908,889 to 39,104,545. A third party candidate, H. Ross Perot, garnered 19,742,267 votes. Bush's defeat has been blamed on a lackluster campaign, and he was badly damaged after breaking his pledge: "Read my lips: No new taxes."

THIRTY-THREE

International Corporate Aid for Marxist-Leninist Communism

One of the strangest paradoxes in the fight against communism has been the help provided by Western international banks and corporations. The Chief Executive Office apparently decided that the bottom line of the annual financial report was more important than the security of their own country and lives in the free world. U.S. administrations from Roosevelt to Carter hardly opposed trade with the Soviet Union, and, in fact, a number actually encouraged trade even though the cold war was in full swing.

The following statement is attributed to Lenin:

> The Capitalists of the world and their governments, in pursuit of conquest of the Soviet market, will close their eyes to the indicated higher reality and thus will turn into deaf mute blind men. They will extend credits which will strengthen for us the Communist Party in their countries and giving us the materials and technology we lack, they will restore our military industry, indispensable for our future victorious attacks on our suppliers. In other words, they will labor for preparation for their own suicide.

The extent of support Western capitalists, and particularly those in the United States, have afforded the Soviet Union since the 1917 Bolshevik Revolution is astounding. The Ford Gorki "Automobile" Plant agreement was signed in May 1929. Construction was completed in 1933 by the Austin Company for production of the Ford Model-A passenger cars and light trucks. In the 1980s the plant was called "Gorki" and produced GAZ automobiles, trucks, and military vehicles. By the late 1930s, production at Gorki was 80,000 to 90,000 Russian Ford vehicles per year. The Ford-Gorki plant has a history of production of armored and wheeled vehicles for Soviet army use, including those used against the United States in Korea and Vietnam.

In 1961, the Department of Commerce approved export by the Bryant Chucking Grinder Company of thirty-five Centalign B machines for processing miniature ball bearings. This shipment, which took place in the early 1970s, brought the capacity of the Soviet Union up to fifty percent of the U.S. capacity and enabled the Soviet Union to close the nuclear missile gap by allowing the Soviet Union to deploy 7,100 multiple independently guided re-entry vehicles (MIRVs).

In 1973, Control Data Corporation agreed to supply the Soviets with a wide range of scientific and engineering information, including construction and design of a large, fast computer, and in 1985, the Soviets were able to establish a plant for producing semi-conductors on a mass scale. Without the semi-conductor capability, the Soviets would have lagged behind in up-grading their military equipment.

Perhaps the largest single project built in Russia by the Western capitalists was the KAMAZ-Kama River integrated heavy duty truck plant. This plant, the largest in the world, is spread over thirty-six square miles situated on the Kama River. It has a capacity to produce over 100,000 multi-axle ten ton trucks, trailers, and off-road vehicles. This deal took place under President Nixon and National Security Advisor Henry Kissinger, and was approved even though the plant had military capability. The Soviet Union invaded Afghanistan with about 85,000 troops beginning on Christmas 1979, using vehicles and other equipment manufactured in the KAMAZ-Kama river integrated heavy duty truck plant. President Amin of

Afghanistan was executed on 27 December 1979, and was replaced by Babrak Karmal, an Afghan Communist in exile under Soviet protection.

One hundred sixty companies traded with the Soviet Union between 1960 and 1985, and this trade was encouraged by both the Democratic and Republican administrations. The products and services offered by these 160 companies included advanced computers, machine tools, electronics, chemicals, drilling equipment, boiler technology, gas technology, aircraft, atomic energy, and non-ferrous metals.

Political and financial assistance may even have been rendered to Lenin and the Soviet Union during the Bolshevik Revolution. Assistance may have come from a number of Wall Street firms during the Revolution itself, including intervention in Washington by prominent bankers and businessmen on behalf of the new Bolshevik regime. During the period 1917 to 1945, more than 100 companies were involved with the Soviet Union in receiving concessions, engaging in technical assistance contracts, or providing Western engineers and experts for specific assignments.

From 1945 to 1970, international banks and international corporations continued to render financial and technical assistance to the Soviet Union with very little opposition from their respective governments. The Soviets began a massive plant purchasing program in the late 1950s. In the United States, for example, the Soviets bought at least fifty complete chemical plants between 1959 and 1963 for chemicals not previously produced in the USSR. A gigantic ship purchasing program was instituted so that by 1967 about two thirds of the Soviet merchant fleet had been built in the West. A little more difficulty was met in the acquisition of computers and similar advanced technologies, but a gradual weakening of Western export controls under persistent Western business and political pressure produced a situation by the end of the 1960s whereby the Soviets were able to purchase almost the very largest and fastest of Western computers (i.e., Control Data).

In the late 1960s, U.S. foreign policy leaders inaugurated "détente" and "Mutual Assured Destruction" programs, which opened the gates for the Soviets to reach parity and then superiority in conventional and nuclear armaments.

I am sure it was most confusing to many of our government officials and members of Congress to watch the tremendous outlays for a national defense designed primarily to protect us from the threatening Soviet Union during the cold war, while at the same time watching our own corporations and banks enter into trade with and loans to the Soviet Union which helped the Soviet Union reach military parity with us.

The International Monetary Fund and the World Bank, which the American Treasury helps to finance with taxpayer assistance, were the forefront of providing loans, at low rates, to the Soviet Union and its captured "Satellite Communist Allies" during the cold war.

I am concerned that we are making the same mistakes with Red China that were made all through the cold war with the Soviet Union. In 1960, Red China broke with the Soviet Union in an ideological dispute, claiming that the Soviet Union was revising Marxism-Leninism and becoming soft in its fight for world domination. In other words, the Chinese Communists were willing to break the monolithic Soviet control over the world Communist movement because they felt the Soviets were no longer capable of properly leading the fight for world Communist domination.

After President Nixon reopened the long-closed door to mainland China with his good will trip there in February 1972, Western corporations and banks tried to go into Red China to make a buck, just like they did in the Soviet Union. But China is a difficult revenue for foreign investors. Bureaucratic hassles, retail problems, cultural differences, and the presence of the Communist leadership hamper efforts at developing a free market. But foreign investment has nonetheless grown rapidly, and in 1985, 1300 overseas firms invested in China. Three major U.S. firms, Boeing, IBM, and Occidental Petroleum, invested over $6 billion.

In a 1991 speech, the General Secretary of the Chinese Communist party warned that, "We must maintain the people's democratic dictatorship led by the working class and based on the worker-peasant alliance. We should not weaken or negate Communist Party leadership, nor should we ever practice a Western style multi-party system." Mao Tse Tung may be dead, but he is clearly not forgotten.

As to the CPC, the general secretary pointed out, "The Chinese Communist Party will, as always, uphold Marxism-Leninism and Mao Tse Tung thought in leading the Chinese people forward along the road of building socialism with Chinese characteristics." The general secretary stressed the importance of democratic centralism as follows, noting that it

> is our Party's fundamental organization principle. Our Party Constitution stipulates that individual party members are subordinate to the Party organization, the minority is subordinate to the majority, the lower Party organizations are subordinate to the higher.

Communism is far from dead in Red China. If we continue our present efforts of helping to build up the Chinese Communist regime, are we facing the possibility of a long cold war with China just as we did with the Soviet Union? We could set forth a long list of human rights violations, for example, but these do not keep our government from renewing China's most favored nation trading status.

Encouraging news that Red China might be losing its Mao revolutionary fervor began to appear in 1985. A "leadership shuffle" was afoot, causing a major shake-up of the Politburo, Central Committee, and other groups. Importance of the shake-up is underscored by the number of officials and the high level of the organizations that are involved. The 131 resignations and retirements, including 64 of the Central Committee's 344 full or alternate members, 37 members of the 162 member Central Advisory Commission, and 30 of 132 members of the Party's Discipline and Inspection Commission, a politically influential group, will be replaced.

> For all his immense influence, Deng Ziaoping, China's paramount leader, has not yet guaranteed a new era for China. But the diminutive reformer has again exercised enough muscle to keep his country headed down roads no other Communist nation ever has traveled.

Some things in China have not changed. As of October 1996, the People's Republic of China was still giving out harsh sentences to dissidents. According to a report in the Fort Myers, Florida, *News Press*, Wang Dan, one of the last active leaders of the 1989 Tiananmen Square democracy movement, was sentenced to eleven years in prison. His trial in Beijing Intermediate People's Court took place amid the usual secrecy and unusually heavy police presence. No foreign reporters or observers were allowed to attend, despite requests by the United States and other governments. Police cordoned off the courthouse in western Beijing, stringing up white rope to keep foreign reporters and curious locals away. Dozens of uniformed and plain clothes police patrolled the area. Wang's writings and meetings were used as evidence to convict him of plotting to subvert the government. The newspaper report concluded that officers confiscated videotapes from at least two foreign cameramen and detained for seven hours a three-man crew from ABC television.

Deng Ziaoping, China's leader, died on 19 February 1997. Deng had seized power in China through a coup in the 1970s allegedly with dreams of modernizing China's economy while opening society. His dreams for China ended during the fateful weekend in Tiananmen Square, when he and other leaders stopped on the road to political reform and decided to turn back. Deng saw his Electric Revolution, die when students and sympathetic freedom protesters were killed as the People's Liberation Army stormed Beijing's giant central square.

Deng's death is not expected to cause any great shifts in Chinese policy. At the moment, China's "sun" is president and Communist Party Chief Jiang Zemin. Jiang has remained on top during a period that saw Beijing's turn to nationalism to consolidate political control. China's current leaders are hard-liners who, according to the U.S. State Department's 1997 Human Rights Report, have stamped out all dissent among China's 1.2 billion people.

Soviet leader Khrushchev (1956-1964) threatened to bury us and thereafter escalated the cold war by bringing on the Cuban missile crisis in 1963. The People's Republic of China survived the cold war and remains a Marxist-Leninist totalitarian regime of 1.2 billion people. The mindset of the present military leaders of China should be of considerable concern to U.S. government leaders. Our country needs the best of all intelligence sources to determine what is really going on inside mainland China.

APPENDIX A

Communist Party USA Organizational Structure

In 1929, the CP USA for the first time became a monolithic party, and it is now appropriate to discuss the organizational and geographical structure of the party.

The National Convention is the highest authority of the CP USA. Constitutionally, it meets once every two years, and its purpose is setting up the Communist line for the ensuing two years. During the Comintern years, the draft of the National Convention's deliberations was sent to Moscow prior to approval by the convention. This was provided for by the Communist International's theses and statutes. The National Convention is also responsible for the election of new officers, including a national chairman and general secretary. The general secretary is regarded as the titular leader of the party.

A National Board is elected by the National Committee. In June 1947, the National Board was composed of twelve members. The National Board is charged with the responsibility of carrying out decisions and the work of the National Committee between sessions.

The National Committee is organized for the purpose of acting on matters affecting the Communist party line during an emergency, and it serves for the National Convention when the latter is not in session. Its composition is determined by the National Convention. The National Committee organizes and supervises departments and committees and commissions, with the exception of the National Review Commission. It guides and directs all political and organizational work of the party.

The National Committee directs and supervises the party press. It administers the National Treasury. It organizes and directs all undertakings of importance to the party. The National Committee meets at least three times a year.

The National Review Commission is elected by the National Convention. To be eligible for membership, a person must have been a member of the party for at least five years. Special commissions are designed to suggest policy changes in order to build up Communist strength in special fields. In 1947, the party had the following commissions in operation: Trade Union, Membership, Education, Women's Commission, Negro Commission, Maritime Commission, Press Department, Veteran's Commission, Nationalities Commission, Catholic Commission, Youth Commission, Foreign Affairs Committee, and others.

In the late 1940s, the CP USA was divided into thirty districts numbered from one to thirty-five (with five numbers not used). A district headquarters may cover a portion of one state, one state or several states. The state organization is the organization within a particular state. The city or county organization is made up of sections in a particular town or county. The section is made up of branches in a particular territorial setting, as for example, a particular part of a town. The officers of the section are elected by a meeting of representatives of the various branches.

The club is the lowest part of the Communist party structure and reaches nearest the masses. In the early Communist party history, the club was known as a "cell." Every member of the party must be a member of a club. The club can either be an industrial club or a territorial or neighborhood club.

The industrial club is the means employed by the party of associating together Communists in a given place of employment. Every factory is to be a Communist stronghold. This is necessary in order to tie up production and to bring about a general strike. If there are two or more Communists in a factory, they must form a club and then a branch in order to build the party and agitate on behalf of the everyday needs of men in factories. The territorial (neighborhood) club is a substitute for the shop branch to take care of the Communist party members who are not employed in plants. It is essentially a territorial grouping of the party's members.

Communist party membership is open to any resident of the U.S. eighteen years of age or over, regardless of race, color, national origin, sex, or religious belief, who subscribes to the principles and purposes of the Communist party.

APPENDIX B

Conditions of Admission to the Communist International

1920

The first Constituent Congress of the Communist International did not draw up precise conditions of admission to the Third International.

At the moment of the convocation of the First Congress in the majority of countries, only Communist currents and groups existed.

The Second World Congress of the Communist International is convening under different conditions. At the present moment in most countries there are not only Communist tendencies and groups but Communist parties and organizations.

The Communist International more and more frequently receives applications from parties and groups which a short time ago belonged to the Second International, but are now desirous of joining the Third International, although they are not yet really Communist. The Second International is completely broken. Seeing the complete helplessness of the Second International, the intermediary faction and the groups of the "centre" are trying to lean on the ever strengthening Communist International, hoping at the same time, however, to preserve a certain "autonomy" which should enable them to carry on their former opportunist or "centrist" policy. The Communist International has become the fashion.

The desire of certain leading groups of the "centre" to join the Third International now is an indirect confirmation of the fact that the majority of conscious workers of the whole world is growing stronger every day.

The Communist International is being threatened with dilution due to the fluctuating and half and half groups which have not as yet abandoned the ideology of the Second International.

It must be mentioned that in some of the large parties (Italy, Norway, Jugo-Slavia, etc.), the majority of which adhere to the point of view of communism, there is up to this moment a considerable reformist and social pacifist wing, which is only awaiting the moment to revive and to begin an active "sabotage" of the proletarian revolution, and thus assist the bourgeoisie and the Second International.

No Communist should forget the lesson of the Hungarian Soviet Republic.

In view of this, the Second World Congress finds it necessary to establish definite conditions for the joining of new parties and to point out these conditions to such parties as have already joined the Communist International. The conditions are as follows:

1. The general propaganda and agitation should bear a very Communist character, and should correspond to the program and decisions of the Third International. The entire party press should be edited by reliable Communists who have proved their loyalty to the cause of the proletarian revolution. The dictatorship of the proletariat should not be spoken of simply as a current hackneyed formula; it should be advocated in such a way that its necessity should be apparent to every rank and file working man and woman, to each soldier and peasant, and should emanate from everyday facts systematically recorded by our press day by day.

All periodicals and other publications, as well as all party publications and editions, are subject to the control of the presidium of the party, independently of whether the party is legal or illegal. The editors should in no way be given an opportunity to abuse their autonomy and carry on a policy not fully corresponding to the policy of the party.

Whenever the followers of the Third International have access, and whatever means of propaganda are at their disposal, whether the columns of newspapers, popular meetings, labor unions or cooperatives, it is indispensable for them not only to denounce the bourgeoisie, but also its assistants and agents, reformists of every color and shade.

2. Every organization desiring to join the Communist International shall be bound systematically and regularly to remove from all the responsible posts in the labor movement (party organizations, editors, labor unions, parliamentary factions, co-operatives, municipalities, etc.), all reformists and followers of the "centre," and to have them replaced by Communists, even at the cost of replacing at the beginning experienced men by rank and file working men.

3. The class struggle in almost every country of Europe and America is entering the phase of civil war. Under such conditions the Communists can have no confidence in bourgeois laws. They should create everywhere a parallel illegal apparatus and in every way possible assist the revolution. In every country where, in consequence of martial law or of other exceptional laws, the Communists are unable to carry on their work lawfully, a combination of lawful and unlawful work is absolutely necessary.

4. A persistent and systematic propaganda and agitation is necessary in the army, where Communist groups should be formed in every military organization. Wherever, owing to repressive legislation, agitation becomes impossible, it is necessary to carry on such agitation illegally. But, refusal to carry on or participate in such work should be considered equal to treason to the revolutionary cause, and incompatible with affiliation with the Third International.

5. A systematic and regular propaganda is necessary in the rural districts. The working class can gain no victory unless it possesses the sympathy and support of at least part of the rural workers and of the poor peasants, and unless other sections of the population are equally utilized. Communist work in the rural districts is acquiring a predominant importance during the present period. It should be carried on through Communist working men of both city and country who have connections with the rural districts. To refuse to do this work, or to transfer such work to untrustworthy half reformists, is equal to renouncing the proletarian revolution.

6. Every party desirous of affiliating with the Third International should renounce not only avowed social patriotism, but also the falsehood and the hypocrisy of social pacifism; it should systematically demonstrate to the workers that without a revolutionary overthrow of capitalism, no international arbitration, no talk of disarmament, no democratic reorganization of the League of Nations will be capable of saving mankind from new Imperialist wars.

7. Parties desirous of joining the Communist International must recognize the necessity of complete and absolute rupture with reformism and the policy of the "centrists," and must advocate this rupture amongst the widest circles of the party membership, without which condition a consistent Communist policy is impossible. The Communist International demands unconditionally and peremptorily that such rupture be brought about with the least possible delay. The Communist International cannot reconcile itself to the fact that such avowed reformists as Turati, Modigliani, Kautsky, Hillquit, Longuet, Macdonald, and others should be entitled to consider themselves members of the Third International. This would make the Third International resemble the Second International.

8. In the colonial question and that of the oppressed nationalities, there is necessary an especially distinct and clear line of conduct of the parties of countries where the bourgeoisie possesses such colonies or oppresses other nationalities. Every party desirous of belonging to the Third International should be bound to denounce without any reserve all the methods of its own Imperialists in the colonies, supporting not only in words but practically a movement of liberation in the colonies. It should demand the expulsion of its own Imperialists from such colonies, cultivate among the working men of its own country a truly fraternal attitude towards the working population of the colonies and oppressed nationalities, and carry on a systematic agitation in its own army against every kind of oppression of the colonial population.

9. Every party desirous of belonging to the Communist International should be bound to carry on systematic and persistent Communist work in the labor unions, co-operatives, and other labor organizations of the masses. It is necessary to form Communist groups within the organizations, which by persistent and lasting work should win over labor unions to communism. These groups should constantly denounce the treachery of the social patriots and of the fluctuations of the "centre." These Communist groups should be completely subordinated to the party in general.

10. Any party belonging to the Communist International is bound to carry on a stubborn struggle against the Amsterdam "International" of the yellow labor unions. It should propagate insistently amongst the organized workers the necessity of a rupture with the yellow Amsterdam International. It should support by all means in its power the international Unification of Red Labor Unions, adhering to the Communist International which is now beginning.

11. Parties desirous of joining in the Third International shall be bound to inspect the personnel of

their parliamentary factions, to remove all unreliable elements therefrom, to control such factions, not only verbally but in reality, to subordinate them to the Central Committee of the party, and to demand from each proletarian Communist that he devote his entire activity to the interests of real revolutionary propaganda.

12. All parties belonging to the Communist International should be formed on the basis of the principle of democratic centralization. At the present time of acute civil war, the Communist party will be able to do its duty only when it is organized in a sufficiently thorough way, when it possesses an iron discipline, and when its party centre enjoys the confidence of the members of the party, who are to endow this centre with complete power, authority, and ample rights.

13. The Communist parties of those countries where the Communist activity is legal should make a clearance of their members from time to time, as well as those of the party organizations, in order to systematically free the party from the petty bourgeois elements which penetrate it.

14. Each party desirous of affiliating with the Communist International should be obliged to render every possible assistance to the Soviet Republics in their struggle against all counter-revolutionary forces. The Communist parties should carry on a precise and definite propaganda to induce the workers to refuse to transport any kind of military equipment intended for fighting against the Soviet Republics, and should also by legal or illegal means carry on a propaganda amongst the troops sent against the workers' republics, etc.

15. All those parties which up to the present moment have stood upon the old social and democratic programs should, within the shortest time possible, draw up a new Communist program in conformity with the special conditions of their country, and in accordance with the resolutions of the Communist International. As a rule, the program of each party belonging to the

Communist International should be confirmed by the next congress of the Communist International or its Executive Committee. In the event of the failure of the program of any party being confirmed by the Executive Committee of the Communist International, the said party shall be entitled to appeal to the Congress of the Communist International.

16. All the resolutions of the congresses of the Communist International, as well as the resolutions of the Executive Committee, are binding for all parties joining the Communist International. The Communist International, operating under the conditions of most acute civil warfare, should be centralized in a better manner than the Second International. At the same time, the Communist International and the Executive Committee are naturally bound in every form of their activity to consider the variety of conditions under which the different parties have to work and struggle, and generally binding resolutions should be passed only on such questions upon which such resolutions are possible.

17. In connection with the above, all parties desiring to join the Communist International should alter their name. Each party desirous of joining the Communist International should bear the following name: Communist Party of such and such a country, section of the Third Communist International. The question of the renaming of a party is not only a formal one, but is a political question of great importance. The Communist International has declared a decisive war against the entire bourgeois world, and all the yellow Social Democratic parties. It is indispensable that every rank and file worker should be able clearly to distinguish between the Communist parties and the old official Social Democratic or Socialist parties, which have betrayed the cause of the working class.

18. All the leading organs of the press of every party are bound to publish all the most important docu-

ments of the Executive Committee of the Communist International.

19. All those parties which have joined the Communist International, as well as those which have expressed a desire to do so, are obliged in as short a space of time as possible, and in no case later than four months after the Second Congress of the Communist International, to convene an extraordinary congress in order to discuss these conditions. In addition to this, the central committees of these parties should take care to acquaint all the local organizations with the regulations of the Second Congress.

20. All those parties which at the present time are willing to join the Third International, but have so far not changed their tactics in any radical manner, should, prior to their joining the Third International, take care that not less than two thirds of their committee members and all of their central institutions should be composed of comrades who have made an open and definite declaration prior to the convening of the Second Congress as to their desire that the party should affiliate with the Third International. Exclusions are permitted only with the confirmation of the Executive Committee of the Third International. The Executive Committee of the Communist International has the right to make an exception also for the representatives of the "centre" as mentioned in paragraph seven.

21. Those members of the party who reject the conditions and the theses of the Third International are liable to be excluded from the party.

This applies principally to the delegates at the special congress of the party.

APPENDIX C

Captive Nations as of 1982

President Ronald Reagan, on 19 July 1982, made his proclamation of Captive Nations Week before 200 people in the White House Rose Garden. He referred to the "old and new" Captive Nations, those made part of the official Union of Soviet Socialist "Republics" before and during World War II, the East Bloc nations dominated by the Kremlin in post-war Europe, and such other late entries as Cuba, Nicaragua and Angola. President Reagan in his remarks called for a new resolve to resist slavery.

The following is a list of the Captive Nations, carefully prepared by the Captive Nations Committee as of 1982. It shows the name of the country and the first year of Communist domination:

Russia	1917
Armenia (Soviet part)	1920
Azerbaidzhan (Soviet part)	1920
Byelorussia (White Russia)	1920
Cossackia	1920
Georgia	1920
Idel-Ural	1920
North Caucasia	1920
Ukraine	1920
Far Eastern Republic	1922
Turkestan	1922
Mongolia	1924
Estonia	1940
Latvia	1940
Lithuania	1940

Albania	1946
Bulgaria	1946
Yugoslavia	1946
Poland	1947
Romania	1947
Czechoslovakia	1948
Korea (North)	1948
Hungary	1949
Germany (East)	1949
China (Mainland part)	1949
Tibet	1951
Vietnam (North)	1954
Cuba	1960
Cambodia	1975
Laos	1975
Vietnam (South)	1975
Angola	1975
Ethiopia	1977
Afganistan	1978
Nicaragua	1979

APPENDIX D

Damage to U.S. Intelligence Agencies Endangers National Security

by Herman O. Bly
3 June 1979

Our country's internal security shield has suffered appalling damage over the past five years. Jefferson's declaration "Eternal vigilance is the price of liberty" should be calling for immediate remedial action and explanation. The startling fact is that we Americans continue to ignore this damage. One reason for this is that we the people have not been properly informed by our press, radio, and television. Another reason is our elected and appointed national representatives have misjudged the people's natural need for a strong national security shield.

Here are the facts which you may be reading for the first time:

In April 1973, the Internal Security Division of the Department of Justice was abolished. In June 1973, the Subversive Activities Control Board was dismantled. In 1974, the U.S. attorney general's list of subversive organizations was eliminated. On 14 January 1975, the House Internal Security Committee was abolished. In 1977, the Senate Internal Security Subcommittee of the Judiciary was eliminated as a separate group.

Meanwhile, further actions were being launched seriously limiting the effectiveness of our key national defense agencies—FBI, CIA, Defense Intelligence Agency (DIA), and the National Security Agency (NSA).

During May-June 1973, under pressure, the CIA dismissed hundreds of senior officers with anti-subversive expertise. Since 1973 many irreplaceable CIA foreign service officers have been forced into early retirement. Shortage of experienced officers is one of the reasons for publicized failures of the CIA in such areas as Iran, Ethiopia, Afghanistan, and Angola.

In 1975, the intelligence community was especially distraught over the drawn out open hearings by the Senate Select Committee headed by Senator Church and the House Special Committee headed by Representative Pike. The principal targets of these highly publicized hearings were our FBI and CIA. These hearings dealt further injury to our overall intelligence gathering capabilities by painting the operations of these agencies with a distorted and sullied image.

The final report of the Church Committee, despite its weaknesses and departure from fact, has been accepted by some legislators and their staff members as a compilation of basic truth concerning the operations of our FBI and our other U.S. intelligence agencies. The report has been used as a platform on which to create controls and restrictions which ultimately would stifle the efforts of our government to protect itself against internal and external enemies who observe no controls and who are subject to no restrictions.

In March 1976, then Attorney General Edward Levi imposed new domestic security guidelines, making it virtually impossible for our FBI to have an effective internal security capability. The Levi guidelines prohibit our FBI from probing any group at all unless it has evidence the organization has violated a federal statute or was planning a violation that threatened great harm and was likely to take place in the near future. On 22 September 1976, then FBI Director Clarance Kelley revealed that because of these guidelines our FBI had been forced to reduce its security cases from 21,414 in July 1973 to a total of 626 cases which included 78 organizations and 548 individuals. Current FBI Director William Webster was reported in the 29 January 1979, *U.S. News & World Report* as saying, "That as a result of these guidelines, literally hundreds of investigations of the past had been closed." Webster said that the FBI was currently investigating between twelve and sixteen domestic organizations and from forty to sixty individuals engaged in terrorist activity.

The subcommittee on criminal laws and procedures of the Senate Judiciary Committee prepared a report in late 1978 which was entitled *The Erosion of Law Enforcement Intelligence and Its Impact On the Public Security*. This report says in no uncertain terms that the U.S. law enforcement and investigative groups no longer had the authority to investigate and/or gather information on those persons or groups who pose an imminent danger to the security of the United States and its citizens. Police departments all over the country are reportedly destroying their so-called intelligence files and disbanding their special departments engaged in developing information on dangerous individuals and organizations who might be involved in terrorist or anarchist-type activities. Apparently these officials have been convinced they do not have the authority to investigate until the bomb has exploded, the public official has been assassinated, or until the anti-government rally becomes an actual riot resulting in bloodshed.

FBI morale really began to plummet following the prosecution of John Kearney, former New York office supervisor of Squad forty-nine. Kearney retired from the FBI in 1972 after twenty-five years service with an immaculate record and the respect and affection of his colleagues. In 1977, five years after his retirement, Kearney was called before a federal grand jury on charges made by officials of the Civil Rights Division of the Department of Justice who had long been hostile to the

FBI. Kearney was indicted on five separate counts for his activities involved in an intensive manhunt to apprehend federal fugitives connected with the Weather Underground Organization, the most vicious group of terrorists yet to operate in America. They were responsible for many bombings, including the U.S. Capitol, the Pentagon, and a number of police headquarters, which resulted in the death of at least one police officer and injury to many others.

Kearney's use of special investigative techniques were similar to those which had been regularly performed by hundreds of other FBI agents for over forty years under the approval of five different presidents. One year after Kearney's indictment and his expenditure of $157,000 in legal and related costs, the Department of Justice dismissed the indictment because it finally recognized it had no case. The department has so far refused to reimburse Kearney for any of his staggering defense costs. It was John Kearney whose civil rights were violated rather than the friends and relatives of the Weather Underground fugitives.

Admittedly, the intelligence community, unlike Caesar's wife, has not been completely pure. However, we have overreacted in crippling our intelligence capabilities. It's past time that we restore the effectiveness and morale of our intelligence agencies so that our people will again provide these agencies with the support, faith, and confidence which they so badly need and deserve.

It is now past time for more Americans to tell our political leaders to get off the backs of our FBI, CIA, and our other national defense agencies and to recognize the obvious fact that our country is in more imminent danger today from a more powerful enemy than at any time in its history. If you believe that we should defend ourselves against our enemies, inside and out, with strong effective intelligence efforts, tell your elected officials.

The above article was written by Herman O. Bly, the first guest columnist for a column called "Operation

Appendix D

Listen" which appeared in the 3 June 1979 issue of the Fort Myers, Florida *News-Press*. This guest editorial was awarded the George Washington Honor Medal in 1979 by the Freedoms Foundation at Valley Forge. This award was considered an outstanding achievement for dedication toward bringing about a better understanding of the "American Way of Life."

EPILOGUE

This book would not be complete without further commentary on my activities in warning against Marxist-Leninist communism after my retirement from government service.

During my twenty-three years of service in the FBI, I received seventeen letters of commendation and one meritorious award. My retirement party was held at 5:00 P.M. on 12 August 1963 in the same large room in the Department of Justice Building where eight Nazi saboteurs were tried. Director J. Edgar Hoover attended. I do not recall that Director Hoover had ever attended a retirement party for any employee less than an assistant director, so I felt honored that he attended. A total of 132 FBI employees attended and signed my retirement book. I was presented with a matched set of Wilson K-28 golf clubs. The following Saturday morning, I used these new clubs and shot a par seventy-two round of golf at the Country Club of Fairfax where I had been a member since 1956.

In September 1963, I received a telephone call from the Central Intelligence Agency (CIA) suggesting that I drop by the CIA Headquarters and meet with Dr. Lothar Metzle. This I did. Metzle offered me a position as Senior Staff Officer in his unit called the Communist International Group (CIG) under a five year contract. My pre-employment security investigation was satisfactory and I began work in December 1963. Dr. Metzle occasionally jokingly referred to me as "Mr. CP USA." I enjoyed my five years of service at the CIA very much, but when it came time for a renewal of my five year contract in December 1968, the Johnson administration was having considerable trouble with its balance of payments. Agencies were facing cutbacks, and several hundred CIA employees were walking the halls at CIA headquarters trying to find a spot to work after coming from abroad. Contracts were not being renewed, and it was with regret that I left the CIA.

My service in the CIA was interesting. In the spring of 1965, I was sent to Mexico City to review all the files on Soviet personnel in Mexico which were located at the U.S. Embassy. I spent thirty days determining from the known activities of each person and to what extent he or she may have been engaged in espionage activities. When I returned to CIA headquarters in McLean, Virginia, I prepared an eighty-five page monograph that was used as a training manual for CIA agents assigned to Latin American countries in contact with Soviet activities.

During the course of my review of the files on Soviet personnel, I ran across the following information that related to Lee Harvey Oswald and the November 1963 assassination of President John F. Kennedy. I was somewhat startled to learn that when Oswald was arrested in Dallas in November 1963, he was asked if he wanted an attorney. Oswald reportedly replied, "Yes, I want attorney Abt." It turns out that John Abt was the New York City attorney who Oswald understood was counsel for the CP USA. Abt reportedly never returned the call. Colonel Rudolf Abel, a suspected key Soviet KGB agent was arrested in New York City on 21 June 1957. At the time of Abel's arrest, much espionage evidence was located in his room at the Hotel Latham. When he was arrested he also reportedly indicated he wanted attorney Abt. Colonel Abel was convicted of espionage and served his prison sentence until 1962, when he was exchanged for U-2 pilot Francis Gary Powers after long negotiations by attorney James Donovan.

When Oswald visited the Soviet Embassy in Mexico City in 1963, the man he went to see was the Soviet official in charge of issuing visas. This seemed quite reasonable, as the excuse Oswald gave for visiting the

Embassy was to obtain a visa to visit Cuba. The irony of this situation is that the Soviet official in charge of issuing visas was also the KGB Soviet espionage agent reportedly connected with KGB Department thirteen activities, which included assassinations.

The third thing that intrigued me about the Oswald case was the fact that this young former U.S. Marine was able to bring his Russian wife home from the Soviet Union when colonels and other American businessmen reportedly were unable to bring their Russian wives back to the U.S. Why was Oswald allowed this special treatment?

The above information worried me, and when I got back to CIA Headquarters, I prepared a memo for the CIA official who had been liaison with the Warren Commission. The Warren report concluded that Lee Harvey Oswald acted as a lone assassin, but I believe the heads of the FBI, CIA, and President Johnson wanted the Oswald case brought to a conclusion as fast as possible as they did not want another crisis with the Soviet Union so soon after the 1963 Cuban missile crisis.

After leaving government service in December 1968, I did not lose my fervor in the fight against atheistic Marxist-Leninist communism. I kept on speaking out against this menace. I have given many lectures including the 9 September 1968 lecture at a meeting of the Arlington, Virginia Lions Club at the Washington Golf & Country Club; the 12 January 1971 lecture before the Rotary Club of McLean, Virginia; 7-28 November 1971 a series of four lectures at the Cherrydale United Methodist Church, Arlington, Virginia; the 30 January 1973 lecture at a meeting of the Bethesda, Chevy Chase Rotary Club at the Kenwood Country in Bethesda, Maryland; the 26 April 1974 lecture before the Methodist Men's Group of Wesley Memorial United Methodist Church, Ft. Myers, Florida; the 26 March 1975 lecture at a meeting of the Forever Young Group of Wesley Memorial United Methodist Church, Ft. Myers, Florida; and the 27 January 1976 lecture at a meeting of the Methodist Men's Club of the First United Methodist Church, Ft. Myers, Florida. This lecture, "Communism vs. Christianity in a Turbulent World," caused quite a stir, and afterward the men voted unanimously for me to put this lecture into pamphlet form for dissemination. This lecture was also awarded the George Washington Honor Medal in 1976 by the Freedoms Foundation at Valley Forge, Pennsylvania.

On 6 November 1976, I lectured at a meeting of the Caloosa Chapter, Sons of the American Revolution, in Cape Coral, Florida; on 11 January 1977, I lectured at a meeting of the Ft. Myers, Florida, Caloosa Lions Club on "Communism vs. Religion," which was a revision of my earlier lecture "Communism vs. Christianity in a Turbulent World." I had this lecture printed and made hundreds of copies available at my expense. I sent copies to eleven U.S. senators, four U.S. congressmen, a number of key syndicated columnists, and to various organizations. In 1977, this lecture received the Valley Forge Honor Certificate Award from the Freedoms Foundation at Valley Forge, Pennsylvania.

On 25 February 1977, I lectured at a meeting of the Cape Coral, Florida High Twelve Club; 15 April 1977, I lectured at a meeting of the Pennsylvania Keystone Club at the Tice Community Club in Ft. Myers, Florida; 11 May 1977, I lectured at a meeting of the Kiwanis Club of Ft. Myers, Florida; 12 April 1978, I lectured to the Fisherman's Class at the First Presbyterian Church in Ft. Myers, Florida; 2 May 1978, I lectured to the Ft. Myers High Twelve Club #423; 8 September 1978, I lectured to the Kiwanis Club of Ft. Myers, Beach, Florida, Division 11, Florida District; 29 November 1978, I lectured to the Rotary Club of Cape Coral, Florida, District 696; 8 February 1979, I lectured to men of the First Presbyterian Church of Port Charlotte, Florida; 15 March 1979, I lectured to the Methodist Men of the United Methodist Church of Cape Coral, Florida; and on 3 June 1979, after I made several complaints to the publisher and editor of the *Fort Myers News Press* that their newspaper was not giving balanced reporting to conservative view points, I received a telephone call from Homer Pyle, editor of the editorial page. He advised me that after considerable discussion, the *Fort Myers News Press* management had decided to launch a new weekly column entitled "Operation Listen." It was decided that I was to be the first columnist and that my column would be published as written and would not be censored in any way. I entitled my 1,000 word column, "Damage to U.S. Intelligence Agencies Endangers National Security." This article appeared on 3 June 1979 and won the 1979 George Washington Honor Medal in the national awards program of the Freedoms Foundation at Valley Forge, Pennsylvania. My fraternity, Sigma Nu Phi (Legal), carried this article in a special edition of its publication, *The Adelphia*. The *Fort Myers News Press* carried only two more weekly columns of "Operation Listen" before abandoning this special column. The full text of my award-winning article is printed in the appendix of this book.

On 5 January 1981, I was the speaker at the monthly meeting of the Lee County United Methodist Men. My speech covered the trial of former FBI officials W. Mark Felt and Edward S. Miller. On 5 May 1981, I lectured at the Seven Lakes Men's Association in Ft. Myers, Florida; on 27 October 1981, I lectured at the United Methodist Men's meeting at the First United Methodist Church in Ft. Myers, Florida; from 31 January 1985 to November 1986, a weekly conservative newspaper was launched in southwest Florida entitled *Lee Constitution,* In January 1985, I was invited to be a columnist, along with such well known writers as Walter E. Williams, Ph.D., Peter Beckman, Ph.D., Rev. D. James Kennedy, Ph.D., Joseph Sobron, Charley Reese, and Paul Harvey. I wrote a total of fifty-four articles for this publication before it was forced to cease publication for financial reasons. It reached a circulation of 45,000. My first twenty articles were published in a pamphlet entitled *America at the Crossroads*. This pamphlet won a national award from the Freedoms Foundation at Valley Forge, Pennsylvania: the Valley Forge Honor Certificate for Excellence in the category of Published Works.

On 12, 19, and 26 June 1986, I delivered three lectures over Christian radio station WSOR (95 FM) in Ft. Myers, Florida. On 13 January 1987, I lectured to the Golden Gate Women's Club at the Community Center in Golden Gate, Naples, Florida; on 26 March 1987, I lectured to the Southwest Florida Chapter of The Association of Former Intelligence Officers at the Palm River Country Club in Bonita Springs, Florida.

On 21 May 1987, I lectured to the Thomas Edison Chapter #10 of the Reserve Officers Association of the U.S. at a meeting in Ft. Myers, Florida; on 17 September 1987, I lectured to the Ft. Myers Chapter of Eagle Forum. In April, May, and June 1988, my lecture "America at the Crossroads" was published in the magazine *SMI* (*Sound Money Investor*). This magazine was then being published quarterly by Millionaire's Manual Inc., a publicly traded corporation in Cocoa, Florida. In October and November 1988, my article "Is the Soviet Threat for Real" was published in the *Sound Money Investor* magazine, in Winter Park, Florida. On 11 October 1989, I lectured before the Ft. Myers Republican Women's Club Federation at the Ramada Inn, Ft. Myers, Florida. This was my last lecture due to my wife's ill health.

In September 1989, my wife, Martha, began to have serious heart trouble and she was hospitalized six times between September 1989 and June 1990. She had a stroke on 10 June 1990, while in the hospital, which left her unable to stand or walk and with considerable speech impairment. As of this date, I am taking care of her in our home in Fort Myers with the help of four nurses. We celebrated our sixtieth Anniversary on 31 July 1997.

The book that I am now writing I hope will fill a void. It will provide all the information Americans need

Epilogue

to know about the history and evils of Marxist-Leninist communism. It identifies many who knowingly aided or were duped or coerced into helping this enemy of democracy and all religions. The prosecution and conviction of the leaders of the CP USA in open court gave indisputable testimony that they were under discipline of the International Communist Movement and enemies of the USA and American way of life.

As a long-time active member of the Methodist Church, I became especially distraught over the fact that a ten million member church organization as late as 1972 had failed to register any real concern about atheistic communism or distress that Marxist-Leninist communism was in control of one fourth of the land mass and one third of the people of the earth. On 5 June 1972, as a member of the Commission on Social Concerns of the Cherrydale United Methodist Church of Arlington, Virginia, I wrote to the headquarters of the Board of Christian Social Concerns of the United Methodist Church in Washington, D.C. I pointed out in my letter that our commission had carefully reviewed the proceedings of the general conference of the United Methodist Church in Atlanta, Georgia held 17-28 April 1972. What we found shocking was the fact that nowhere during the twelve day conference was there any open expression of dismay or protest against atheistic communism. I asked for a reply which might throw some light on the matter. Six weeks later, I finally received a reply, dated 21 July 1972, from the assistant general secretary to the board. He enclosed a twenty-two page pamphlet entitled *Social Principles of the United Methodist Church*, adopted by the 1972 general conference in Atlanta, Georgia. A paragraph of his letter reads as follows:

> Your concern for an expression against Communism as an atheistic force was expressed in one of the petitions and was written into a report which was placed before the entire general Conference,

but it was defeated on a floor vote, in favor of the statement which was adopted on Indochina.

I immediately wrote back of 22 July 1972:

> Nowhere in this twenty-two page pamphlet (which sets forth for public record the social principles of the United Methodist Church) is there any mention or concern for the persecuted Christians trying to practice their religious beliefs inside Communist countries. This omission should weigh heavily on the conscience of truly dedicated Methodist leaders and particularly members of your Board. I am particularly disillusioned over the negative attitude of the Board of Christian Social Concerns of the Methodist Church toward militant atheistic Communism. Your letter of July 21st has helped to increase rather than allay my disillusionment.

The assistant general secretary wrote back on 3 August 1972. One paragraph of his letter is particularly cogent:

> The fact that we do affirm our faith in God and in Christ as Savior (as recorded in the preamble to the Social Principles) seems to me the basis upon which we judge all other ideologies and all other efforts to control life, and to restrict freedoms rather than to enlarge them. Therefore, I believe it is our responsibility to do all that we can to further the gospel of Christ and to try in a positive way to achieve justice an peace in the world, rather than building up walls which separate people more and more.

After several more contacts with the assistant general secretary, he arranged for me to meet on 16 January 1973, with the top five board members of the Church and Society Commission of the church. The luncheon meeting was held in a separate dining space of the Supreme Court Building cafeteria. After lunch I spoke for forty-five minutes on the subject of atheistic communism and its threat to all organized religions, stressing the point that the Methodist Church should play a more important role in the world wide cold war instigated by Marxist-Leninist communism. Following my remarks, the spokesman for the board briefly advised that by the year 2000 we would have nothing to fear from communism, as there would be peace and freedom throughout the world. I was amazed at this reaction to my remarks. None of the other board members offered any comments. It was apparent I had failed to change the minds of the top policymakers of the United Methodist Church.

My next effort to reach the leadership church was through the Methodist weekly newspaper, *The Texas Methodist-The United Methodist Reporter,* published in Dallas, Texas. On 23 May 1975, I sent the following letter to the editor:

> To the Editor:
>
> This paper, as the official church publication in Florida, is in my opinion, constantly mixing up its social concern priorities when selecting topics for discussion and publication. Recent issues of your publication have carried an abundance of articles which, by their tone, slant and prominence, seem to call for sympathy and or acceptance of homosexuality. Other articles seem to play up attacks on our basic American institutions such as a recent article which publicized a church women's group attack on the FBI. I could go on *ad nauseum.*
>
> It would seem to me that with one-third of the people of the earth and one fourth of the land surface of the globe languishing under the yoke of Godless Communist dictatorships, that sooner or later, the Methodist press would point out that the tenets of Communism represent the very antithesis of the principles of Christianity. Why not just once remind your readers that Marxist-Leninist dogma teaches all Communists to believe, among other things that: "Nature is all—there is no God;

> The body is all—there is no soul; All religions are false and harmful they must be destroyed."
>
> At the April 1972 General Conference of the United Methodist Church in Atlanta, GA., not one resolution was passed condemning the persecution of Christians and other practicing religionists in the Communist controlled countries.
>
> If the Methodist press does not face up to its responsibilities, I doubt very much if the United Methodist Church will allow even a discussion of the persecution of Christians in Communist lands at its next General Conference in Portland, Oregon in April 1976. It would appear, on the other hand, that homosexuality will be a prominent topic for discussion at that conference.
>
> I have been an active Methodist for more than fifty years and am becoming more and more disillusioned.
>
> Herman O. Bly
>
> Ft. Myers, FL.

On 6 June 1975, I received a reply from the editor indicating that my letter was being set in type and would be published, space permitting. On 26 July 1975 and again on 20 September 1975, I wrote the editor and complained that my letter of 23 May, had not yet been published. Finally, on 21 November 1975, my letter was published in the *United Methodist Reporter.* I wrote the editor and thanked him for running my letter. I added the sentence: "I sincerely hope that you will include more articles on Christian-Communism issues in the future."

Still upset over the failure of the Methodist Church to recognize the atheistic Communist threat throughout the world, I sent the following letter on 1 August 1976 to the editor of *The Texas Methodist, The United Methodist Reporter,* in Dallas, Texas:

> You will recall that in February and March 1976, we exchanged correspondence relating to the per-

secution of Christians and believers in the Soviet Union and other Communist dominated countries following my sending you a copy of my lecture "Communism vs. Christianity in a Turbulent World," which I had given before a group of Methodist men in Ft. Myers, FL. on January 27, 1976.

As you know, I have been quite critical of the leadership of the United Methodist Church for not showing concern for the persecution of Christians inside Communist controlled countries. In fact, just as I had predicted, at the General Conference of the United Methodist Church, held in Portland, Oregon, In April-May 1976, the Church leaders thought it much more important to discuss homosexuality and other issues than to take time to discuss or show sympathy for Christian believers who are being persecuted for practicing their religious beliefs by Communist governments controlled by atheistic leaders.

What prompts this letter is to call to your attention that the United Methodist Church leaders and yourself have now lost the great opportunity to have been the first strong voice to show concern for the growing persecutions of Christian believers in Communist countries.

Enclosed is an article which appeared in the July 3, 1976 issue of, *The Washington Post* entitled "Movement Grows in Congress for Soviet Christian Support," which points out that Rep. John Buchanan (R. AL.) has 103 co-sponsors in the House including most of the leadership, for his resolution calling on the Soviet government to allow Christians and other religious believers to 'worship God freely according to their own conscience."

Also enclosed is a copy of an article entitled "Religious Persecution in Soviet Union Probed," which appeared in the August 11, 1976, issue of the Fort Myers "News Press" which points out that the policy making body of the World Council of Churches met on August 10th to discuss and to consider religious freedom in the light of a ninety-two page report charging that the Soviet government continues to persecute religious believers.

Members of Congress and leaders of the World Council of Churches are taking action which the United Methodist Church leadership should have taken a long time ago and which even today they appear not ready to discuss.

You, as the Editor of the Great Methodist publication, should consider taking some action on this matter. Please take some time to read again my lecture, 'Communism vs. Christianity in a Turbulent World." A copy is enclosed.

Sincerely yours,

Herman O. Bly

On 8 February 1977, I wrote again to the editor of the, *Texas Methodist*. The first paragraph of my letter reads as follows:

> I want to take this opportunity to thank you and your staff for the editorial, "We should seek to insure human right's everywhere—including USSR' which you carried in the December 17, 1976 issue of, the *Texas Methodist*. This is a great step forward.

Finally, this book is my last effort to relate the story behind the story regarding the true nature of Marxist-Leninism and make Americans aware of the serious threat that still exists from this Communist menace. I sincerely hope it will help prevent the leadership of our government, our religious bodies, and our great industrial international corporations from repeating the mistakes that were made during the cold war of 1945 to 1991. I sincerely hope we will not have to go through a long cold war with the People's Republic of China, which is still a Marxist-Leninist-Maoist Communist dictatorship with 1.2 billion inhabitants.

BIBLIOGRAPHY

Barron, John, *Operation Solo—The FBI's Man in the Kremlin*, (Washington, DC: Regnery Publishing Inc., 1997), 367.

Committee on Internal Security, *The Theory and Practice of Communism, Part II*, (Washington, DC: U.S. House of Representatives, 1973) 375.

de Toledano, Ralph, *The Greatest Plot in History* (New Rochelle, NY: Arlington House Publisher, 1963), 306.

Digest of the Public Record of Communism in the United States, (New York City: Fund for the Republic, 1955), 753.

Fundamentals of Marxism-Leninism (Moscow: Foreign Languages Publishing House, 1961), 891.

Internal Security Manual (Revised), Provisions of Federal Statutes, Executive orders and congressional resolutions relating to the Internal Security of the U.S. (Washington DC: U.S. Government Printing Office, 1961), 496.

Gill, William J., *The Ordeal of Otto Otepka* (New Rochelle, NY: Arlington House, 1969), 505.

Hoover, J. Edgar, *Masters of Deceit* (New York: Henry Holt & Co., Publisher, 1958), 374.

Hoover, J. Edgar, *J. Edgar Hoover on Communism*, (New York: Random House, Publisher, 1969) 157.

Hoover, J. Edgar, *A Study of Communism* (New York: Holt, Rinehart & Wilson, Publisher, 1962) 211.

Hosty, James P., *Assignment Oswald* (New York: Arcade Publishing, 1996), 328.

Klehr, Harvey and John Earl Haynes, *The American Communist Movement, Storming Heavens Itself* (New York: Scribners Reference, Publisher, 1992), 210.

Lamphere, Robert J. and Tom Shachtman, *The FBI— KGB War, A Special Agent's Story* (New York: Random House, Publisher, 1986), 320.

Morris, Robert, *Our Globe Under Siege II* (Mantoloking, NJ: J & W Enterprises, Publisher, 1988) 200.

Powers, Richard Gid, *Not Without Honor* (New York: The Free Press, Publisher, 1995), 554.

Solzhenitzyn, Aleksandr I., *The Gulag, Archepelago* (New York: Harper & Row, Publisher, 1973), 660.

Steibel, Gerald L., *Détente: Promises and Pitfalls*, (New York: Cranke, Russak & Co., Inc., Publisher, 1975), 85.

Sung an, Tai, *Mao Tse-tung's Cultural Revolution* (Pegasus, Division of Bobbs-Merrill Co., Publisher, 1972), 211.

Sutton, Dr. Anthony C., *The Best Enemy Money Can Buy* (Billings, MT: Liberty House, Publisher, 1986) 261.

Unger, Sanford J., *FBI An Uncensored Look Behind the Walls* (New York: Little Brown & Co., Publisher, 1975) 682.

Communism and the New Left (Washington, DC: U.S. News & World Report, 1969), 222

Walt, General Lewis W. U.S.M.C., Retired, *The Eleventh Hour* (New York: Caroline House Inc., Publisher, 1979) 100.

Welch, Robert, *The Politician* (Belmont, MA: Belmont Publishing Co., 1963), 295.

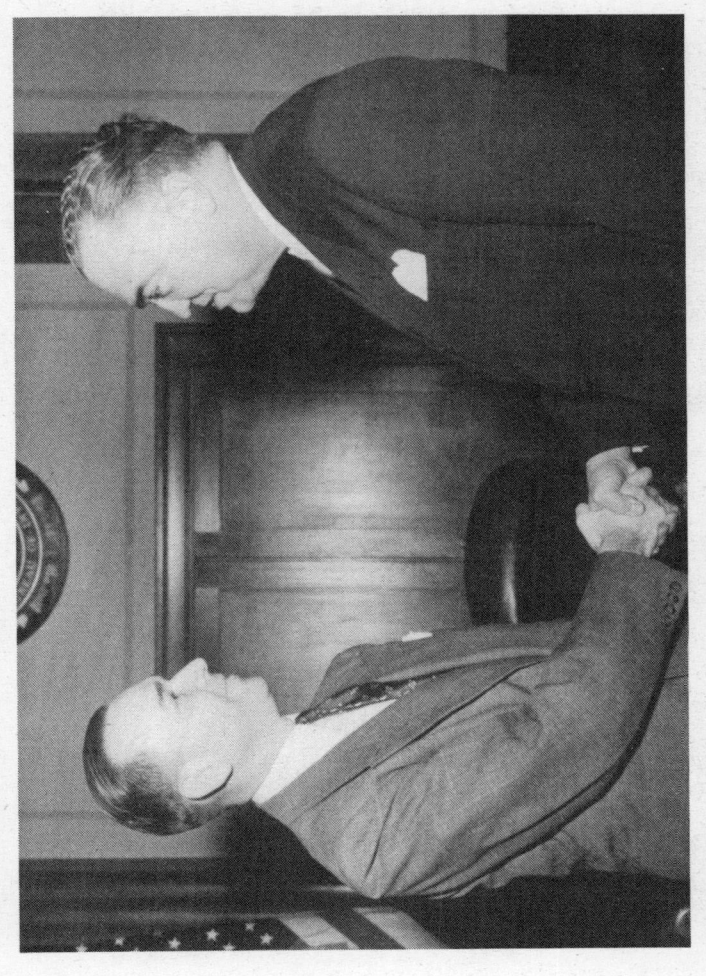

Herman O. Bly being presented a meritorious award on 28 January 1953 by J. Edgar Hoover (Director of FBI) in his office

Domestic Intelligence Division, FBI, 20th Anniversary in FBI, 8/12/60 (L-R) Fred J. Baumgardner, Chief Internal Security Section, FBI, Martha B. Bly, wife of Herman O. Bly, Herman O. Bly, Alan H. Belmont, Asst. Director, Domestic Intelligence Division, FBI

Martha B. Bly and Herman O. Bly
20th Anniversary at FBI headquarters
8/12/60

J. Edgar Hoover, Director of FBI, sends photo upon retirement of Herman O. Bly on 8/12/63.